D0452779

BTEC Level 3 National Study Skills Guide in Construction

Welcome to your Study Skills Guide! You can make it your own – start by adding your personal and course details below...

Learner's name: _____

BTEC course title: _____

Date started: _____

Mandatory units:

_____

_____

_____

Optional units:

_____

_____

_____

Centre name: _____

Centre address:

_____

_____

_____

Tutor's name: _____

Published by Pearson Education Limited, a company incorporated in England and Wales, having its registered office at Edinburgh Gate, Harlow, Essex, CM20 2JE. Registered company number: 872828

Edexcel is a registered trademark of Edexcel Limited

Text © Pearson Education Limited 2010

First published 2010

13 12 11 10

10 9 8 7 6 5 4 3 2 1

British Library Cataloguing in Publication Data

A catalogue record for this book is available from the British Library

ISBN 978 1 84690 560 5

Copyright notice

All rights reserved. No part of this publication may be reproduced in any form or by any means (including photocopying or storing it in any medium by electronic means and whether or not transiently or incidentally to some other use of this publication) without the written permission of the copyright owner, except in accordance with the provisions of the Copyright, Designs and Patents Act 1988 or under the terms of a licence issued by the Copyright Licensing Agency, Saffron House, 6–10 Kirby Street, London EC1N 8TS (www.cla.co.uk). Applications for the copyright owner's written permission should be addressed to the publisher.

Typeset and edited by Ken Vail Graphic Design, Cambridge
Cover design by Visual Philosophy, created by eMC Design
Cover photo/illustration © Corbis/Artiga Photo
Printed in Malaysia, KHL-CTP

Acknowledgements

The author and publisher would like to thank the following individuals and organisations for permission to reproduce photographs:

Alamy Images: Angela Hampton Picture Library 19, Image Source 53, Claudia Wiens 58; **Corbis:** 68, Stephanie Carter 45/2, Archive / CAS Images 45; HSE: 44/5; **iStockphoto:** 44/3, 45/3, 46/2, Lukasz Laska 76, Sean Locke 46, Chris Schmidt 33; **Pearson Education Ltd:** Steve Shott 28, Ian Wedgewood 51; Pearson Education Ltd: Gareth Boden 44, Corbis 7, Photodisc 44/2; **Photolibrary.com:** sodapix sodapix 10; **Science Photo Library Ltd:** Stevie Grand 44/4; **Shutterstock:** Ford Photography 46/3, Yobidaba 45/4

Cover images: *Front:* **Corbis:** Artiga Photo

All other images © Pearson Education

Every effort has been made to contact copyright holders of material reproduced in this book. Any omissions will be rectified in subsequent printings if notice is given to the publishers.

Websites

Go to www.pearsonhotlinks.co.uk to gain access to the relevant website links and information on how they can aid your studies. When you access the site, search for either the title BTEC Level 3 National in Construction or ISBN 9781846905605.

Disclaimer

This material has been published on behalf of Edexcel and offers high-quality support for the delivery of Edexcel qualifications.

This does not mean that the material is essential to achieve any Edexcel qualification, nor does it mean that it is the only suitable material available to support any Edexcel qualification. Edexcel material will not be used verbatim in setting any Edexcel examination or assessment. Any resource lists produced by Edexcel shall include this and other appropriate resources.

Copies of official specifications for all Edexcel qualifications may be found on the Edexcel website: www.edexcel.com

Contents

BLACKBURN COLLEGE
LIBRARY
Acc. No. BB57720
Class No. 690 TOP
Date .... FEB 14

Popular progression pathways

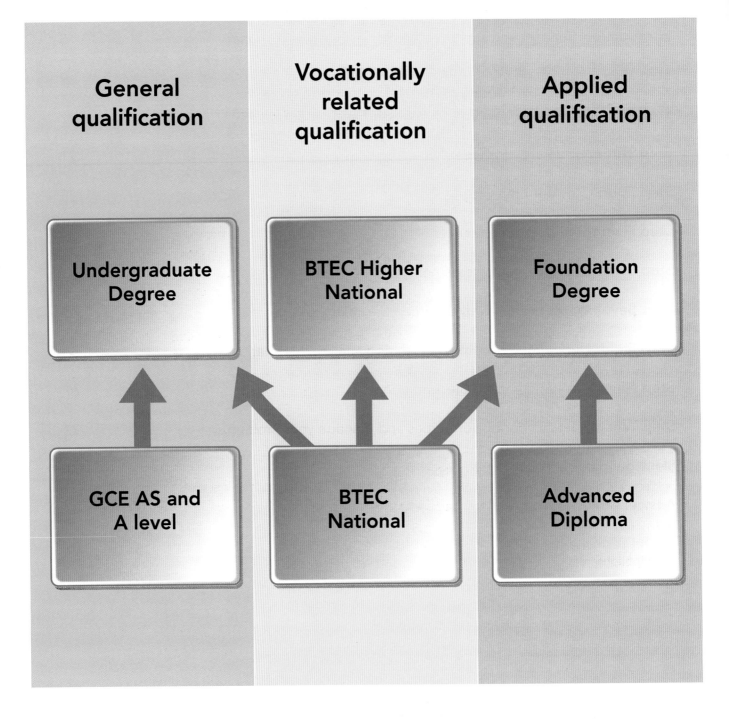

General qualification

Vocationally related qualification

Applied qualification

Undergraduate Degree

BTEC Higher National

Foundation Degree

GCE AS and A level

BTEC National

Advanced Diploma

Ten steps to success in your BTEC Level 3 National

This Study Skills Guide has been written to help you achieve the best result possible on your BTEC Level 3 National course. At the start of a new course you may feel both quite excited but also a little apprehensive. Taking a BTEC Level 3 National qualification has many benefits and is a major stepping stone towards your future career. Using this Study Skills Guide will help you get the most out of your course from the start.

TOP TIP

Use this Study Skills Guide at your own pace. Dip in to find what you need. Look back at it whenever you have a problem or query.

During **induction** sessions at the start of your course, your tutor will explain important information, but it can be difficult to remember everything and that's when you'll find this Study Skills Guide invaluable. Look at it whenever you want to check anything related to your course. It provides all the essential facts you need and has a Useful terms section to explain specialist terms, words and phrases, including some that you will see highlighted in this book in bold type.

This Study Skills Guide covers the skills you'll need to do well in your course – such as managing your time, researching and analysing information and preparing a presentation.

- Use the **Top tips** to make your life easier as you go.
- Use the **Key points** to help you to stay focused on the essentials.
- Use the **Action points** to check what you need to know or do now.
- Use the **Case studies** to relate information to your chosen sector and vocational area.

- Use the **Activities** to test your knowledge and skills.
- Use the **Useful terms** section to check the meaning of specialist terms.

This Study Skills Guide has been designed to work alongside the Edexcel Student Book for BTEC Level 3 National Construction (Edexcel, 2010). This Student Book includes the main knowledge you'll need, with tips from BTEC experts, Edexcel assignment tips, assessment activities and up-to-date case studies from industry experts, plus handy references to your Study Skills Guide.

This Study Skills Guide is divided into ten steps, each relating to a key aspect of your studies, from understanding assessment to time management to maximising opportunities. Concentrate on getting things right one step at a time. Thousands of learners have achieved BTEC Level 3 National qualifications and are now studying for a degree, or building a successful career at work. Using this Study Skills Guide, and believing in your own abilities, will help you achieve your future goals, too.

Introduction to the construction sector

You are entering a complex and wide-ranging industry which forms a major part of the UK's economic and social wealth. The UK construction industry covers many areas including:

- civil engineering
- construction
- refurbishment
- adaptation
- services.

This course will give you a valuable insight into the construction industry and will allow you to grasp the breadth of its activities, the services that it provides, and the different personnel involved at craft, technical and professional level. You will learn about the complexity of the industry and the roles of the people involved in design and construction teams, including their responsibilities for completing a contract on time, to budget and within quality control boundaries.

We all need buildings; to provide shelter from the elements, as places to work and locations to relax and socialise. The range of buildings we encounter is vast, from the London Olympic Stadium to the house that you live in.

Also included in this industry is the maintenance of the built environment. All buildings have a life cycle which might include a repair programme or update plan to improve technology and finishes, for example utilising advances in glass technology.

Construction is not just restricted to the UK; it is a global industry. Many professionals train within the UK then choose to work abroad in countries where many high quality construction projects are developed, for example the Persian Gulf. Your potential on your chosen career pathway is determined by the amount of effort and motivation that you put into your studies. It is up to you to get the most from your BTEC course.

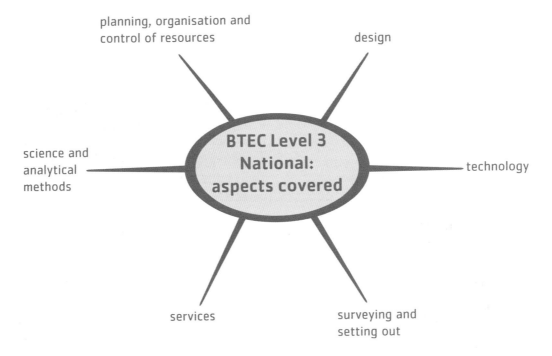

The various aspects of construction covered by the BTEC Level 3 National qualification.

Case study: Where will your BTEC National take you?

Kris's career aspiration was to enter the teaching profession.

He attended his local school and managed to achieve 6 GCSEs at grade C. He went on to take two A-levels but failed the exams. This result meant he did not feel confident following the academic route.

Kris attended his local Further Education College open evening where he signed up for the National Diploma in Construction. He was attracted by the learning style of the course.

The two-year course extended his skills and knowledge in construction such that he entered University and after four years of study gained a first class honours degree in Construction Management, a great achievement.

Kris went on to work for a national contractor as a Quantity Surveyor before becoming a lecturer at a further education college. He also ran a successful business designing small extensions for local clients for planning regulation approvals.

The BTEC National in Construction started Kris on a journey that allowed him to achieve great successes in his life, more than he could have dreamed.

How will you achieve your dreams?

A BTEC Level 3 National in Construction could open up a career in quantity surveying for you.

Skills for your sector

Practical skills

Some of the setting out and surveying units involve not only an element of theoretical knowledge, but also its practical application in a fieldwork assessment. This assessment may include the collection of accurate linear and levelling information, and the measurement of angles using surveying instruments.

Using this information to produce detailed drawings is another skill required for the practical element of the course (see below).

In surveying you will use various skills that include:

- accurate recording
- note taking
- graphical detailed drawings
- mathematical skills
- sketching.

Graphical skills

Certain units of the programme will require you to develop skills in producing drawn information. Initially, you will work on paper to hone your skills. You may then advance to use a computer and display screen with digital media such as Google Sketchup or AutoCAD.

When developing drawing skills you need to be:

- clean and tidy
- accurate
- able to select and use the right media
- capable of presenting information correctly.

Team working

Your tutor may frequently ask you to work within a team or small group. This could involve getting on with people you don't know. Don't forget, this situation is just like a construction site where you would also be expected to work with people that you have not met before. The skills that are required when working within a team are:

- listening
- speaking
- leading
- following instructions
- consulting others
- presenting information
- problem solving
- negotiating
- pulling together to compete with other teams.

Other skills

Time management, research, presentation and writing skills are also important in your BTEC Level 3 National course. You will learn more about these in this Study Skills Guide.

Step One: Understand your course and how it works

Case study: Finding out more about the course

Having left school at 16, Simon has enrolled on the BTEC Level 3 National Diploma in Construction at his local further education college. He is unsure of what the course is about. He attended an introductory event at the end of the summer term, but that was three months ago.

Simon arrives on the first day at 10 am as instructed by a letter that was sent to his home. He is apprehensive at first, but recognises a lot of mates from school. The class is given a tour of facilities, followed by a full course induction. This involves informing the students on the course about:

- the unit contents
- methods of assessment
- pass, merit and distinction grades and points tracking
- the assessment schedule and timetable
- student ICT accounts
- institute policies
- how to get help
- contact information for all staff and students
- the location of all rooms and facilities
- travel arrangements.

At the end of his first day, Simon is now fully aware of what is required in order to pass the course and feels that he has a good overview of the course content and the methods of assessment that will be used. Simon also knows who to ask should he require any further information or advice. He has been shown how to access the Edexcel website for further information on the BTEC Nationals in Construction, including how to download the unit specifications. He has also found out how to track his progress towards UCAS points for the Built Environment Degree course he is aiming for. Simon is aware that this vocational course is assessed continually and that working hard will help him to achieve higher grades and greater success.

Reflection points

Think about how much you know about your course right now and if there is anything you still need to find out. To start you off, do you know:

- where to hand in completed assessments
- how many assessments you will need to complete this year
- the policy on handing in work late?

What else do you think you need to know? Do you know where or who to go to in order to obtain this information?

What do you think the benefits might be of studying and working at the same time?

All BTEC Level 3 National qualifications are **vocational** or **work-related**. This means that you gain specific knowledge and understanding relevant to your chosen area. It gives you several advantages when you start work.

For example, you will already know quite a lot about your chosen area, which will help you settle down more quickly. If you are already employed, you become more valuable to your employer.

Your BTEC course will prepare you for the work you want to do.

There are four types of BTEC Level 3 National qualification:
Certificates, Subsidiary Diplomas, Diplomas and Extended Diplomas

	Certificate	Subsidiary Diploma	Diploma	Extended Diploma
Credit	30	60	120	180
Equivalence	1 AS-level	1 A-level	2 A-levels	3 A-levels

These qualifications are often described as **nested**. This means that they fit inside each other (rather like Russian dolls) because the same units are common to each qualification – so you can progress from one to another easily by completing more units.

TOP TIP

The structure of BTEC Level 3 National qualifications means it's easy to progress from one type to another and gain more credits, as well as specialise in particular areas that interest you.

- Every BTEC Level 3 National qualification has a set number of **mandatory units** that all learners must complete.
- All BTEC Level 3 National qualifications include **optional units** that enable you to study particular areas in more depth.

- Some BTEC Level 3 National qualifications have **specialist pathways**, which may have additional mandatory units. These specialist pathways allow you to follow your career aims more precisely. For example, if you are studying to become an IT practitioner, you can choose pathways in Software Development, Networking, Systems Support or IT and Business.

- On all BTEC courses you are expected to be responsible for your own learning. Obviously your tutor will give you help and guidance when necessary but you also need to be 'self-starting' and able to use your own initiative. Ideally, you can also assess how well you are doing and make improvements when necessary.

- BTEC Level 3 National grades convert to UCAS points, just like A-levels, but the way you are assessed and graded on a BTEC course is different, as you will see in the next section.

Key points

- You can study part-time or full-time for your BTEC Level 3 National.

- You can do a Certificate, Subsidiary Diploma, Diploma, or Extended Diploma, and progress easily from one to the other.

- You will study both mandatory units and optional units on your course.

- When you have completed your BTEC course you can get a job (or **apprenticeship**), use your qualification to develop your career and/or continue studying to degree level.

- On all BTEC Level 3 National courses, the majority of your learning is practical and vocationally focused to develop the skills you need for your chosen career.

Using the Edexcel website to find out about your course

- You can check all the details about your BTEC Level 3 National course on the Edexcel website – go to www.edexcel.com.

- Enter the BTEC Level 3 National qualification title in the qualifications finder.

- Now find the specification in the list of documents. This is a long document so don't try to print it. Instead, look at the information on the units you will be studying to see the main topics you will cover.

- Then save the document or bookmark the page so that you can easily refer to it again if you need to.

Action points

1 By discussing with your tutor and by exploring the Edexcel website, find out the key information about your course and use it to complete the 'Important Information' form on the next page. You can refer to this form at any time to refresh your memory about any part of your studies.

a) Check whether you are studying for a BTEC Level 3 Certificate, Subsidiary Diploma, Diploma, or Extended Diploma and the number of units you will be studying.

b) Find out the titles of the mandatory units you will be studying.

c) Find out the titles of the optional units and identify the ones offered at your centre.

d) Check the length of your course, and when you will be studying each unit.

e) Identify the optional units you will be taking. On some National courses you will do this at the start, while on others you may make your final decision later.

f) Find out other relevant information about your BTEC Level 3 National qualification. Your centre may have already given you details about the structure.

g) Ask your tutor to help you to complete point 10 on the form. Depending on your course, you may be developing specific additional or personal skills – such as personal, learning and thinking skills (PLTS) and functional skills – or spending time on work experience, going on visits or doing other activities linked to your subject area.

h) Talk to your tutor about point 12 on the form as your sources of information will depend on the careers guidance and information at your centre. You may find it useful to exchange ideas with other members of your class.

	IMPORTANT INFORMATION ON MY BTEC LEVEL 3 NATIONAL COURSE
1	The title of the BTEC Level 3 National qualification I am studying is:
2	The length of my course is:
3	The total number of units I will study is:
4	The number of mandatory units I have to study is:
5	The titles of these mandatory units and the dates (or terms) when I will study them are:
6	The main topics I will learn in each mandatory unit include:

	IMPORTANT INFORMATION ON MY BTEC LEVEL 3 NATIONAL COURSE
7	The number of optional units I have to study is:
8	The titles of the optional units I will study are:
9	The main topics I will learn in each optional unit include:
10	Other important aspects of my course are:
11	After I have achieved my BTEC Level 3 National my options include:
12	Useful sources of information I can use to find out more about these options include:

2 Many learners already have information, contacts or direct experiences that relate to their course. For example, you may have a specific interest or hobby that links to a unit, such as being a St John Ambulance cadet if you are studying Public Services. Think about the relevant sources of information you already have access to and complete the table below.

MY INFORMATION SOURCES	
Experts I know	(Who they are, what they know)
My hobbies and interests	(What they are, what they involve)
My job(s)	(Past and present work and work experience, and what I did)
Programmes I like to watch	(What these are, how they relate to my course)
Magazines and/or books I read	(What these are, examples of relevant articles)
ICT sources	(My centre's intranet as well as useful websites)
Other	(Other sources relevant for my particular course and the topics I will be studying)

Activity: Your future options

At the beginning of a new course it is helpful to think about what career pathway options may be available to you in the Construction workforce. All assignments and work experience on the programme contribute to your final grade and knowing what you are aiming for will help keep you motivated.

Using a mind map to explore different ideas is a good way to consider the range of options available to you. You will also be able to find out the requirements for each career pathway.

For example, if you wish to work with budgets, costs and finance, you could explore the different routes to becoming a Professional Quantity Surveyor or a main contractor's Quantity Surveyor.

You will find the internet a useful source of information. A good starting point is the website of the Royal Institute of Chartered Surveyors (RICS). Go to page 88 to find out how to access the website for this activity.

Create a mind map on the next page to record your ideas about future career options.

TOP TIP

People usually perform better if they understand why they have chosen, or been asked, to do something.

Career options available to me in Construction

Step Two: Understand how you are assessed and graded

Case study: Working towards a grades goal

Eventually, Mathew wants to go to university to take a Quantity Surveying degree course. He has just started his National Diploma in Construction and has two years to get the results he needs. Through the information and guidance he has been given, Mathew realises that he must get high grades in order to be accepted onto one of the better Built Environment university courses. The more popular universities want the top-level students and require at least a DDD grade as an entrance qualification. Mathew is aware that he has to work hard from day one in order to achieve his goal. To reach his goal, Mathew must:

- stick to the hand-in dates given
- always undertake corrections quickly
- make sure he knows what is required for the higher grades
- plan his workload
- map his points score on a tracking sheet.

Mathew works very hard in the first year and achieves eight distinctions and one merit. He applies to university through UCAS and receives an offer of DMM for the university he really wants to go to. By planning out the rest of the year he realises that, if he sticks to merit grades for the rest of the nine units, he will achieve this result. Mathew decides to try even harder and his final year grades are six distinctions and three merits.

Remember that you will need to manage your time when studying, making sure that you allow sufficient time to get the assessments done and also to relax away from your studies.

Reflection points

Think about your future goals. Do you know what you want to do after you finish your BTEC National in Construction?

If there are certain things that you will require to pursue this goal, eg grade requirements or work experience, what can you start doing now to give yourself the best possible chance of realising your goal?

Your assessment

This section looks at the importance of your assignments, how they are graded and how this converts into unit points and UCAS points. Unlike A-levels, there are no externally-set final exams on a BTEC course. Even if you know this because you already have a BTEC First qualification, you should still read this section as now you will be working at a different level.

Your learning is assessed by **assignments**, set by your tutors. You will complete these throughout your course, using many different **assessment methods**, such as real-life case studies, **projects** and presentations. Some assignments may be work-based or **time-constrained** – it depends very much on the vocational area you are studying.

Your assignments are based on **learning outcomes** set by Edexcel. These are listed for each unit in your course specification. You must achieve **all** the learning outcomes to pass each unit.

TOP TIP

Check the learning outcomes for each unit by referring to the course specification – go to www.edexcel.com.

Important skills to help you achieve your grades include:

- researching and analysing information (see page 55)
- using your time effectively (see page 25)
- working co-operatively as a member of a team (see page 49).

Your grades, unit points and UCAS points

On a BTEC Level 3 National course, assessments that meet the learning outcomes are graded as pass, merit or distinction. The different grades within each unit are set out by Edexcel as **grading criteria** in a **grading grid**. These criteria identify the **higher-level skills** you must demonstrate

to achieve a higher grade (see also Step Six – Understand your assessment, on page 35).

All your assessment grades earn **unit points**. The total points you get for all your units determines your final qualification grade(s) – pass, merit or distinction. You get:

- one final grade if you are taking a Certificate or Subsidiary Diploma
- two final grades if you are taking a Diploma
- three final grades if you are taking an Extended Diploma.

Your points and overall grade(s) convert to **UCAS points**, which you need to be accepted onto a degree course. For example, if you achieve three final pass grades for your BTEC Level 3 Extended Diploma, you get 120 UCAS Tariff points. If you achieve three final distinction grades, this increases to 360 – equivalent to three GCE A-levels.

Please note that all UCAS information was correct at the time of going to print, but we would advise you to check their website for the most up to date information. See page 88 for how to access their website.

Case study: Securing a university place

Chris and Shaheeda both want a university place and have worked hard on their BTEC Level 3 Extended Diploma course.

Chris's final score is 226 unit points, which converts to 280 UCAS Tariff points. Shaheeda has a total score of 228 unit points – just two points more – which converts to 320 UCAS points! This is because a score of between 204

and 227 unit points gives 280 UCAS points, whereas a score of 228 to 251 points gives 320 UCAS points.

Shaheeda is delighted because this increases her chances of getting a place on the degree course she wants. Chris is annoyed. He says if he had realised he would have worked harder on his last assignment to get two points more.

You start to earn points from your first assessment, so you get many benefits from settling in quickly and doing good work from the start. Understanding how **grade boundaries** work also helps you to focus your efforts to get the best possible final grade.

You will be able to discuss your learning experiences, your personal progress and the

achievement of your learning objectives in **individual tutorials** with your tutor. These enable you to monitor your progress and overcome temporary difficulties. You can also talk about any worries you have. Your tutor is one of your most important resources and a tutorial gives you their undivided attention.

You can talk through any questions or problems in your tutorials.

Key points

- Your learning is assessed in a variety of ways, such as by assignments, projects and real-life case studies.

- You need to demonstrate specific knowledge and skills to achieve the learning outcomes set by Edexcel. You must achieve all the grading criteria to pass a unit.

- The grading criteria for pass, merit and distinction are shown in a grading grid for the unit. Higher-level skills are needed for higher grades.

- The assessment grades of pass, merit and distinction convert to unit points. The total unit points you receive for the course determines your final overall grade(s) and UCAS points.

TOP TIP

It's always tempting to spend longer on work you like doing and are good at, but focusing on improving your weak areas will do more to boost your overall grade(s).

Action points

1 Find out more about your own course by carrying out this activity.

a) Find the learning outcomes for the units you are currently studying. Your tutor may have given you these, or you can find them in your course specification – go to www.edexcel.com.

b) Look at the grading grid for the units and identify the way the requirements change for the higher grades. If there are some unfamiliar words, check these in Step Six of this guide (see page 35 onwards).

c) If the unit points system still seems complicated, ask your tutor to explain it.

d) Check the UCAS points you would need for the course or university which interests you.

e) Design a form you can use to record the unit points you earn throughout your course. Keep this up-to-date. Regularly check how your points relate to your overall grade(s), based on the grade boundaries for your qualification. Your tutor can give you this information or you can check it yourself in the course specification.

Activity: Calculating points scores

You will need to use the course specification – available on the Edexcel website www.edexcel.com – and the tariff tables from the UCAS website to answer the questions below. To find out how to access the UCAS website go to page 88.

1 The specification contains a grading grid with point scores for your overall award (see pages 21–22). Answer the following questions

   a How many points do you get for a pass?

   b How many points do you get for a distinction?

   c What is the points range for a DDD grade?

2 When you finish your BTEC National Course, you may want to go on to higher education. If you do not apply before completing your course or do not get good enough grades to take up a place you have been offered, you can go through the UCAS clearing service for all undergraduates. Irrespective of when you apply, if you are offered a place it will probably be based on UCAS points.

Having just completed the BTEC Level 3 National Extended Diploma in Construction, Mustafa is hoping to apply to university. He took 18 10-credit units and the grades he achieved are shown below.

Pass	Merit	Distinction
3	8	7

By using the specification guide from the Edexcel website (see pages 21–22) and the tariff table for BTEC Nationals on the UCAS website, calculate the number of UCAS points Mustafa has earned based on his grades.

3 James has achieved 240 points for his BTEC Level 3 National Diploma. He has received an offer from a university for 360 UCAS points. How much extra work will he have to do to satisfy this requirement?

Step Three: Understand yourself

Case study: Growing in confidence

Angela is writing a personal statement for her university application. While writing this, she reflects on the BTEC Level 3 National in Construction, from the start of the course until the present, nearly at the end.

Angela remembers the start of the course, nearly 18 months ago. She was nervous and apprehensive about what was going to happen; how she would cope with the work and what the outcome would be. She started the course at 16, a bit shy, but making a few friends and tentatively joining in social activities.

Angela has since grown into a confident and capable young person who has no problems speaking out in front of her peers, and who is polite and friendly towards others. She has worked hard and gained nine distinction grades in the first year. She now has a vast understanding of the construction industry and the roles and responsibilities within it, which has helped reinforce her choice of becoming a Professional Quantity Surveyor.

Angela's parents are invited to an open evening to discuss her report. As they talk to her tutor, they are amazed at the changes that have taken place in their daughter. Angela's parents are extremely proud of her progress, which will help her in the Quantity Surveying career she has chosen to follow. As a QS Angela will need to be confident in her ability to challenge work costs and final accounts, and discuss variations on construction projects.

As Angela finishes her personal statement, she comes to the conclusion that the hard work and effort she has put in have been worthwhile, especially as she has had such positive reactions from other people, including her friends, family and tutors.

Reflection points

Think about your own personality and try to be honest with yourself.

What are your weaknesses? How do you think you could work on overcoming them as Angela did?

What are your strengths? How can you put these strengths to good use on your BTEC National course?

Self-awareness means understanding how you 'tick'. For example, do you prefer practical activities rather than theory? Do you prefer to draw or sketch an idea, rather than write about it?

Self-awareness is important as it makes you less reliant on other people's opinions and gives you confidence in your own judgement. You can also reflect on your actions to learn from your experiences.

Self-awareness also means knowing your own strengths and weaknesses. Knowing your strengths enables you to feel positive and confident about yourself and your abilities. Knowing your weaknesses means you know the areas you need to develop.

You can analyse yourself by looking at...

... your personality and preferences

You may have taken a personality test at your centre. If not, your tutor may recommend one to use, or there are many available online.

Many employers ask job candidates to complete a personality test so that they can match the type of work they are offering to the most suitable candidates. Although these tests can only give a broad indication of someone's personality they may help to avoid mismatches, such as hiring someone who is introverted to work in sales.

... your skills and abilities

To succeed in your assignments, and to progress in a career, requires a number of skills. Some may be vocationally specific, or professional, skills that you can improve during your course – such as sporting performance on a Sports course. Others are broader skills that are invaluable no matter what you are studying – such as communicating clearly and co-operating with others.

You will work faster and more accurately, and have greater confidence, if you are skilled and proficient. A quick skills check will identify any problem areas.

TOP TIP

Use the Skills Building section on page 77 to identify the skills you need for your course. You'll also find hints and tips for improving any weak areas.

Key points

- You need certain skills and abilities to get the most out of your BTEC Level 3 National course and to develop your career potential.
- Knowing your strengths and weaknesses is a sign of maturity. It gives you greater confidence in your abilities and enables you to focus on areas for improvement.

TOP TIP

You will find more help on developing your skills and abilities in the sections on: Working as a member of a group; Using time wisely; Researching and analysing information; and Making effective presentations.

Action points

1 Gain insight into your own personality by answering each of the following statements *True* or *False* with a tick. Be honest!

		True	False
a)	If someone annoys me, I can tell them about it without causing offence.		
b)	If someone is talking, I often interrupt them to give them my opinion.		
c)	I get really stressed if I'm under pressure.		
d)	I can sometimes become very emotional and upset on other people's behalf.		
e)	I sometimes worry that I can't cope and may make a mess of something.		
f)	I am usually keen, enthusiastic and motivated to do well.		
g)	I enjoy planning and organising my work.		
h)	I find it easy to work and co-operate with other people and take account of their opinions.		
i)	I am easily influenced by other people.		
j)	I often jump to conclusions and judge people and situations on first impressions.		
k)	I prefer to rely on facts and experience rather than following my instincts.		

Now identify which of the skills and qualities in the box below will be really important in your chosen career.

> tact   truthfulness   listening skills
>
> staying calm under pressure
>
> empathy with others   self-confidence
>
> initiative   planning and organising
>
> working with others   self-assurance
>
> objective judgements

Use your answers to identify areas you should work on to be successful in the future.

2 As part of the UCAS process, all **higher education** applicants have to write a personal statement. This is different from a CV, which is a summary of achievements that all job applicants prepare. You may have already prepared a CV but not thought about a personal statement. Now is your chance to!

Read the information about personal statement in the box. Then answer these questions:

a) Explain why personal statements are so important for higher education applicants.

b) Why do you think it is important for your personal statement to read well and be error-free?

c) Suggest three reasons why you shouldn't copy a pre-written statement you have found online.

d) Check the websites you can access from the hotlink given in the box to see what to include in the statement and how to set it out.

e) Prepare a bullet point list of ten personal facts. Focus on your strengths and good reasons why you should be given a place on the higher education course of your choice. If possible, discuss your list with your tutor. Then keep it safely, as it will be useful if you need to write a personal statement later.

Personal statements

This is the information that all higher education applicants have to put in the blank space on their UCAS form. The aim is to sell yourself to admissions tutors. It can be pretty scary, especially if you haven't written anything like it before.

So, where do you start?

First, *never* copy pre-written statements you find online. These are just for guidance. Even worse are websites that offer to write your statement for a fee, and send you a few general, pre-written paragraphs. Forget them all: you can do better!

Imagine you are an admissions tutor with 60 places to offer to 200 applicants. What will you need to read in a personal statement to persuade you to offer the applicant a place?

Most likely, clear explanations about:
- what the applicant can contribute to the course
- why the applicant really wants a place on your course
- what the applicant has done to further his or her own interests in this area, eg voluntary work
- attributes that show this applicant would be a definite bonus – such as innovative ideas, with evidence eg 'I organised a newsletter which we published every three months …'

A personal statement should be well written, with no grammatical or spelling errors and organised into clear paragraphs.

For further guidance, go to page 88 to find out how to access a number of helpful websites.

Activity: Preparing your personal statement

Personalise the table below with suitable information about yourself and your thoughts which you can use to develop your personal statement.

My interests, hobbies and social activities	
Why this subject interests me	
Why I chose this course	
Why I want to go to university	
Jobs, placements and work experience	

Step Four: Use your time wisely

Case study: Getting the balance right

Jamie has always been a disorganised learner. He did not plan very well for his GCSEs and only just scraped C-grade passes in most of the subjects he took. Now he has gained a place on the BTEC National Diploma in Construction and needs to think about addressing the problems he has faced in the past.

During the first week of the course, the tutor delivers a thorough induction, including a section on work planning. The tutor explains that planning your workload is important to:

- avoid having to do too much work in a short period of time
- provide sufficient time to attain higher grades
- ensure that you hand work in on time
- manage your time outside of timetabled classes effectively.

Jamie has never done any of this, but feels he must in order to succeed in the future – he is hoping to apply to university in January next year. Jamie analyses his timetable for the week and factors in the social events he has arranged for the evenings and weekends. He creates a draft work planner that he can fix to the wall to help him organise the time he will spend working on assessments. Each week he monitors whether he has managed to stick to his plan.

Jamie now realises that this vocational construction course is continually assessed; he must keep ahead with the workload so he doesn't fall behind with his assignments.

Jamie tries to keep up his planning for a month and is surprised to see that he has made improvements in his grades, while still being involved in personal activities, like playing for the football team. He decides to continue planning as it has given him positive results so far.

Reflection points

What do you think this case study reveals about the benefits of planning and being organised?

Think about the approach you currently take to your studies. How good are you at:

- planning your time effectively
- setting yourself targets
- prioritising tasks
- monitoring your progress?

If you need to make improvements in some or all of these areas, how would you go about it?

Most learners have to combine course commitments with other responsibilities such as a job (either full- or part-time) and family responsibilities. You will also want to see your friends and keep up your hobbies and interests. Juggling these successfully means you need to be able to use your time wisely.

This involves planning what to do and when to do it to prevent panics about unexpected deadlines. As your course progresses, this becomes even more important as your workload may increase towards the end of a term. In some cases there could be two or more assignments to complete simultaneously. Although tutors try to avoid clashes of this sort, it is sometimes inevitable.

To cope successfully, you need time-management skills, in particular:

- how to organise your time to be more productive
- how to prioritise tasks
- how to overcome time-wasters.

Organising your time

- **Use a diary or wall chart.**
  Using a different colour pen for each, enter:
  - your course commitments, eg assignment dates, tutorials, visits
  - important personal commitments, eg sports matches, family birthdays
  - your work commitments.

TOP TIP

A diary is useful because you can update it as you go, but a wall chart gives you a better overview of your commitments over several weeks. Keep your diary or chart up-to-date and check ahead regularly so that you have prior warning of important dates.

- **Identify how you currently use your time.**
  - Work out how much time you spend at your centre, at work, at home and on social activities.
  - Identify which commitments are vital and which are optional so you can find extra time if necessary.
- **Plan and schedule future commitments.**
  - Write down any appointments and tasks you must do.
  - Enter assignment review dates and final deadline dates in different colours.
  - This should stop you from arranging a dental appointment on the same morning that you are due to give an important presentation – or planning a hectic social life when you have lots of course work to do.

- **Decide your best times for doing course work.**
  - Expect to do most of your course work in your own time.
  - Work at the time of day when you feel at your best.
  - Work regularly, and in relatively short bursts, rather than once or twice a week for very long stretches.
  - If you're a night owl, allow an hour to 'switch off' before you go to bed.
- **Decide where to work.**
  - Choose somewhere you can concentrate without interruption.
  - Make sure there is space for resources you use, such as books or specialist equipment.
  - You also need good lighting and a good – but not too comfortable – chair.
  - If you can't find suitable space at home, check out your local or college library.
- **Assemble the items you need.**
  - Book ahead to get specific books, journals or DVDs from the library.
  - Ensure you have your notes, handouts and assignment brief with you.
  - Use sticky notes to mark important pages in textbooks or folders.

TOP TIP

Set yourself a target when you start work, so that you feel positive and productive at the end. Always try to end a session when a task is going well, rather than when you are stuck. Then you will be keener to go back to it the next day. Note down outstanding tasks you need to continue with next time.

- **Plan ahead.**
  - If anything is unclear about an assignment, ask your tutor for an explanation as soon as you can.
  - Break down long tasks or assignments into manageable chunks, eg find information, decide what to use, create a plan for finished work, write rough draft of first section, etc.
  - Work back from deadline dates so that you allow plenty of time to do the work.
  - Always allow more time than you need. It is better to finish early than to run out of time.

TOP TIP

If you are working on a task as a group, organise and agree times to work together. Make sure you have somewhere to meet where you can work without disturbing other courses or groups.

- **Be self-disciplined.**
  - Don't put things off because you're not in the mood. Make it easier by doing simple tasks first to get a sense of achievement. Then move on to something harder.
  - Plan regular breaks. If you're working hard you need a change of activity to recharge your batteries.
  - If you have a serious problem or personal crisis, talk to your personal tutor promptly.

TOP TIP

Make sure you know the consequences of missing an assignment deadline, as well as the dispensations and exemptions that can be given if you have an unavoidable and serious problem, such as illness (see also pages 36 and 75).

How to prioritise tasks

Prioritising means doing the most important and urgent task first. Normally this will be the task or assignment with the closest deadline or the one that will most affect your overall course grades.

One way of prioritising is to group tasks into ABC categories.

Category A tasks	These must be done now as they are very important and cannot be delayed, eg completing an assignment to be handed in tomorrow.
Category B tasks	These are jobs you should do if you have time, because otherwise they will rapidly become Category A, eg getting a book that you need for your next assignment.
Category C tasks	These are tasks you should do if you have the time, eg rewriting notes jotted down quickly in a lesson.

Expect to be flexible. For example, if you need to allow time for information to arrive, then send for this first. If you are working in a team, take into account other people's schedules when you are making arrangements.

Avoiding time-wasters

Everyone has days when they don't know where the time has gone. It may be because they were constantly interrupted or because things just kept going wrong. Whatever the reason, the end result is that some jobs don't get done.

If this happens to you regularly, you need to take steps to keep on track.

Some useful tips are:

- **Warn people in advance when you will be working.**
  - Ask them to not interrupt you.
  - If you are in a separate room, shut the door. If someone comes in, make it clear you don't want to talk.
  - If that doesn't work, find somewhere else (or some other time) to work.
- **Switch off your mobile, TV, radio and iPod/MP3 player.**
  - Don't respond to, or make, calls or texts.
  - If someone rings your home phone, let voicemail answer or ask them to call back later.
- **Be strict with yourself when you are working online.**
  - Don't check your email until you've finished work.
  - Don't get distracted when searching for information.
  - Keep away from social networking sites.
- **Avoid displacement activities.**
  - These are the normally tedious jobs, such as cleaning your computer screen, that suddenly seem far more attractive than working!

Talking to friends can occupy a lot of time.

TOP TIP

The first step in managing your own time is learning to say 'no' (nicely!) if someone asks you to do something tempting when you should be working.

TOP TIP

Benefits to managing your own time include being less stressed (because you are not reacting to problems or crises), producing better work and having time for a social life.

Key points

- Being in control of your time allows you to balance your commitments according to their importance and means you won't let anyone down.
- Organising yourself and your time involves knowing how you spend your time now, planning when and where it is best to work, scheduling commitments and setting sensible timescales to complete your work.
- Knowing how to prioritise means you will schedule work effectively according to its urgency and importance. You will need self-discipline to follow the schedule you have set for yourself.
- Identifying ways in which you may waste time means you can guard against these to achieve your goals more easily.

Action points

1 Start planning your time properly.

a) Find out how many assignments you will have this term, and when you will get them. Put this information into your diary or planner.

b) Update this with your other commitments for the term – both work/course-related and social. Identify possible clashes and decide how to resolve the problem.

c) Identify one major task or assignment you will do soon. Divide it into manageable chunks and decide how long to allow for each chunk, plus some spare time for any problems. If possible, check your ideas with your tutor before you put them into your planner.

2 How good are you at being responsible for your own learning?

a) Fill in the following table. Score yourself out of 5 for each area: where 0 is awful and 5 is excellent. Ask a friend or relative to score you as well. See if you can explain any differences.

	Scoring yourself	Other person's score for you
Being punctual		
Organisational ability		
Tidiness		
Working accurately		
Finding and correcting own mistakes		
Solving problems		
Accepting responsibility		
Working with details		
Planning how to do a job		
Using own initiative		
Thinking up new ideas		
Meeting deadlines		

b) Draw up your own action plan for areas where you need to improve. If possible, talk this through at your next **tutorial** (see page 18).

Activity: Planning your time

Complete the work schedule below to show which periods of time you can devote to completing assessments.

Day	Monday	Tuesday	Wednesday	Thursday	Friday	Saturday	Sunday
9–10							
10–11							
11–12							
12–1							
1–2							
2–3							
3–4							
4–5							
5–6							
6–7							
7–8							
8–9							

TOP TIP

Don't waste time doing things that distract you when studying for this course. In the construction business, time costs money.

Step Five: Utilise all your resources

Case study: Resources for the course

Mustafa has enrolled on the BTEC Level 3 National Diploma in Civil Engineering course and will start after the summer. He is preparing for two years of study at his local further education college. During the initial interview, he was told by the course tutor that he will need some basic resources:

- a set of set squares for graphical detailing
- a drawing pen set with bow compass and extension arm
- a scientific calculator
- a 0.5mm clutch drawing pencil with drawing eraser
- masking tape or drawing clips
- the BTEC Level 3 Construction Student Book
- A4 lever arch file with dividers
- assignment folders or plastic wallets
- access to the internet from home with a PC.

The tutor advises that learners can obtain an educational discount on the book and drawing equipment, which will be helpful for Mustafa. He will also need a sturdy bag to carry his notes and equipment to college as he plans to walk in each day.

Mustafa doesn't qualify for the Educational Maintenance Allowance and so will need to get a summer job to save up for the resources. He finds a Saturday job helping out in the yard of a local builders' merchant; he is able to set aside some of his earnings for his college resources.

The job has also given him some experience of working with the materials that are used within the construction and civil engineering industry.

Reflection points

It is important to be organised from the very start of your course. It is helpful to think carefully about how you will manage your filing system for notes, course handouts and any other information. Think about the structure of the course and everything you will need to file.

Now devise a filing system that will work for you and that you will follow throughout your course.

Your resources are all the things that can help you to be successful in your BTEC Level 3 National qualification, from your favourite website to your **study buddy** (see page 32) who collects handouts for you if you miss a class.

Your centre will provide essential resources, such as a library with appropriate books and electronic reference sources, the computer network and internet access. You will have to provide basic resources such as pens, pencils and file folders yourself. If you have to buy your own textbooks, look after them carefully so you can sell them on at the end of your course.

TOP TIPS

PPE is **Personal Protective Equipment**. It is used to give protection against certain physical and chemical hazards.

Here is a list of resources, with tips for getting the best out of them.

- **Course information**. This includes your course specification, this Study Skills Guide and all information on the Edexcel website relating to your BTEC Level 3 National course. Course information from your centre will include term dates, assignment dates and your timetable. Keep everything safely so you can refer to it whenever you need to clarify something.
- **Course materials**. These include course handouts, printouts, your own notes and textbooks. Put handouts into an A4 folder as soon as you get them. Use a separate folder for each unit you study.

TOP TIP

Filing notes and handouts promptly means they don't get lost, will stay clean and uncrumpled and you won't waste time looking for them.

- **Stationery**. You need pens and pencils, a notepad, a hole puncher, a stapler and sets of dividers. Dividers should be clearly labelled to help you store and quickly find notes, printouts and handouts. Your notes should be headed and dated, and those from your own research must also include your source (see Step Eight – page 55 onwards).
- **People**. Your tutors, specialist staff at college, classmates, your employer and work colleagues, your relatives and friends are all valuable resources. Many will have particular skills or work in the vocational area that you are studying. Talking to other learners can help to clarify issues that there may not have been time to discuss fully in class.

A **study buddy** is another useful resource as they can make notes and collect handouts if you miss a session. (Remember to return the favour when they are away.)

Always be polite when you are asking people for information. Prepare the questions first and remember that you are asking for help, not trying to get them to do the work for you! If you are interviewing someone for an assignment or project, good preparations are vital. (See Step Eight – page 55 onwards.)

If someone who did the course before you offers help, be careful. It is likely the course requirements will have changed. Never be tempted to copy their assignments (or someone else's). This is **plagiarism** – a deadly sin in the educational world (see also Step Six – page 35).

TOP TIP

A positive attitude, an enquiring mind and the ability to focus on what is important will have a major impact on your final result.

Key points

- Resources help you to achieve your qualification. Find out what resources you have available to you and use them wisely.
- Have your own stationery items.
- Know how to use central facilities and resources such as the library, learning resource centres and your computer network. Always keep to the policy on IT use in your centre.
- People are a key resource – school or college staff, work colleagues, members of your class, friends, family and people who are experts in their field.

Action points

1 a) List the resources you will need to complete your course successfully. Identify which ones will be provided by your school or college, and which you need to supply yourself.

b) Go through your list again and identify the resources you already have (or know how to access) and those you don't.

c) Compare your list with a friend's and decide how to obtain and access the resources you need. Add any items to your list that you forgot.

d) List the items you still need to get and set a target date for doing this.

2 'Study buddy' schemes operate in many centres. Find out if this applies to your own centre and how you can make the best use of it.

In some you can choose your study buddy, in others people are paired up by their tutor.

- Being a study buddy might mean just collecting handouts when the other person is absent, and giving them important news.

- It may also mean studying together and meeting (or keeping contact by phone or email) to exchange ideas and share resources.

With a study buddy you can share resources and stay on top of the course if you're ever away.

Activity: Using resources

Complete the following table to help you research the different resources you will need. Find out:

- what each resource is
- how much it costs
- where you can get it from.

Resource	Price	Supplier details
0.5mm clutch pencil		
0.5mm & 0.35mm ink pens		
A2 drawing board and t-square		
large bow compass		
BTEC Level 3 National Construction, Building Services Engineering and Civil Engineering Student Book (ISBN 9781846906565)		
scale ruler with scales 1:500 1:1250 1:5 1:20 1:50 1:100		
45° set square		
60° set square		

Step Six: Understand your assessment

Case study: Gaining the marks you need

Liam is in his second year of the BTEC National Diploma in Construction and wants to do well so he can progress onto a university degree. He is aware that the competition for university places is tough, with many able students entering higher education. This means that higher grades are needed for the most popular and over-subscribed universities – which will be looking for distinction-level students to enrol on their top courses.

Liam managed to obtain seven merits and two passes in the first year of the Diploma. Recently, he has received an offer for a place on a really great Civil Engineering degree course; he must obtain a Distinction, Merit, Merit (DMM) award. Liam realises that he must get some distinction grades this year or he will not meet the university entrance requirements.

Liam's tutor has stated that the previous year's grades cannot be revisited as this is against the college's academic code and policy. The tutor has also told him that he could improve his grades just by handing his work in on time. Liam remembers that the penalty for handing work in late is to drop a grade. This means that some of his first-year merit grades could have been distinctions, if he had not been over two weeks late with the assignments.

Remember, the more UCAS points you are able to get, the better your chances of obtaining a place at your first-choice university. Working within deadlines will improve grades. Another tip is to use your vacation time to work for a local construction company; this always looks good on a CV and increases your chances of success.

Reflection points

Liam has dropped grades on his course as a result of handing in work late. Do you know what your centre's policy is for late submissions? Think about the steps you could take to ensure that you always meet assignment deadlines.

It is a good idea to keep track of the grades you achieve as your course progresses, so that you always have a record of attainment for reference. Think about a system you could devise to monitor your performance.

Being successful on any BTEC Level 3 National course means first understanding what you must do in your assignments – and then doing it.

Your assignments focus on topics you have already covered in class. If you've attended regularly, you should be able to complete them confidently.

However, there are some common pitfalls it's worth thinking about. Here are tips to avoid them:

- Read the instructions (the assignment brief) properly and several times before you start.
- Make sure you understand what you are supposed to do. Ask if anything is unclear.

- Complete every part of a task. If you ignore a question, you can't meet the grading criteria.
- Prepare properly. Do your research or reading before you start. Don't guess the answers.
- Communicate your ideas clearly. You can check this by asking someone who doesn't know the subject to look at your work.
- Only include relevant information. Padding out answers makes it look as if you don't know your subject.
- Do the work earlier rather than later to avoid any last-minute panics.
- Pay attention to advice and feedback that your tutor has given you.

TOP TIP

Most learners don't do their best in assessments because of silly mistakes, carelessness and rushed work, rather than through major problems of understanding. Make sure you take the time to plan and understand your assignments.

The assignment 'brief'

This may be longer than its name implies! The assignment brief includes all the instructions for an assignment and several other details, as you can see in the table below.

What will you find in a BTEC Level 3 National assignment brief?	
Content	**Details**
Title	This will link to the unit and learning outcomes
Format/style	Written assignment, presentation, demonstration, etc
Preparation	Read case study, do research, etc
Learning outcomes	These state the knowledge you must demonstrate to obtain a required grade
Grading criterion/ criteria covered	eg P1/M1/D1
Individual/group work	Remember to identify your own contribution in any group work
Feedback	Tutor, peer review
Interim review dates	Dates to see your tutor
Final deadline	Last submission date

TOP TIP

Reading and understanding each assignment brief is vital. Ask your tutor if there's anything you don't understand.

Your centre's rules and regulations

Your centre will have several policies and guidelines about assignments, which you need to check carefully. Many, such as those listed below, relate to Edexcel policies and guidelines.

- The procedure to follow if you have a serious problem and can't meet a deadline. An extension may be granted.
- The penalty for missing a deadline without good reason.
- The penalty for copying someone else's work. This is usually severe, so never share your work (or CDs or USB flash drive) with anyone else, and don't borrow theirs.
- **Plagiarism** is also serious misconduct. This means copying someone's work or quoting from books and websites and pretending it is your own work.
- The procedure to follow if you disagree with the grade you are given.

Understanding the question or task

There are two aspects to a question or task. The first is the **command words**, which are described below. The second is the **presentation instructions**, which is what you are asked to do – don't write a report when you should be producing a chart!

Command words, such as 'explain', 'describe', 'analyse' and 'evaluate' state how a question must be answered. You may be asked to 'describe' something at pass level, but you will need to do more, perhaps 'analyse' or 'evaluate', to achieve merit or distinction.

Many learners fail to achieve higher grades because they don't realise the difference between these words. Instead of analysing or evaluating they give an explanation instead. Adding more details won't achieve a higher grade – you need to change your whole approach to the answer.

The **grading grid** for each unit of your course gives you the command words, so that you know what to do to achieve a pass, merit or distinction. The tables that follow show you what is usually required when you see a particular command word. These are just examples to guide you as the exact response will depend on the question. If you have any doubts, check with your tutor before you start work.

There are two important points to note.

- A command word, such as 'create' or 'explain', may be repeated in the grading criteria for different grades. In these cases the complexity or range of the task itself increases at the higher grades.
- Command words vary depending on your vocational area. So Art and Design grading

- grids may use different command words from Applied Science, for example.

TOP TIP

Look at this section again when you get your first assignment and check the command words against these explanations.

To obtain a pass grade

To achieve a pass you must usually demonstrate that you understand the important facts relating to a topic and can state these clearly and concisely.

Command words for a pass	Meaning
Create (or produce)	Make, invent or construct an item.
Describe	Give a clear, straightforward description that includes all the main points and links these together logically.
Define	Clearly explain what a particular term means and give an example, if appropriate, to show what you mean.
Explain … how/why	Set out in detail the meaning of something, with reasons. It is often helpful to give an example of what you mean. Start with the topic then give the 'how' or 'why'.
Identify	Distinguish and state the main features or basic facts relating to a topic.
Interpret	Define or explain the meaning of something.
Illustrate	Give examples to show what you mean.
List	Provide the information required in a list rather than in continuous writing.
Outline	Write a clear description that includes all the main points but avoid going into too much detail.
Plan (or devise)	Work out and explain how you would carry out a task or activity.
Select (and present) information	Identify relevant information to support the argument you are making and communicate this in an appropriate way.
State	Write a clear and full account.
Undertake	Carry out a specific activity.
Examples:	
Identify the main features on a digital camera.	
Outline the steps to take to carry out research for an assignment.	

To obtain a merit grade

To obtain a merit you must prove that you can apply your knowledge in a specific way.

Command words for a merit	Meaning
Analyse	Identify separate factors, say how they relate to each other and how each one relates to the topic.
Classify	Sort your information into appropriate categories before presenting or explaining it.
Compare and contrast	Identify the main factors that apply in two or more situations and explain the similarities and differences or advantages and disadvantages.
Demonstrate	Provide several relevant examples or appropriate evidence which support the arguments you are making. In some vocational areas this may also mean giving a practical performance.
Discuss	Provide a thoughtful and logical argument to support the case you are making.
Explain (in detail)	Provide details and give reasons and/or evidence to clearly support the argument you are making.
Implement	Put into practice or operation. You may also have to interpret or justify the effect or result.
Interpret	Understand and explain an effect or result.
Justify	Give appropriate reasons to support your opinion or views and show how you arrived at these conclusions.
Relate/report	Give a full account, with reasons.
Research	Carry out a full investigation.
Specify	Provide full details and descriptions of selected items or activities.
Examples: Compare and contrast the performance of two different digital cameras. Explain in detail the steps to take to research an assignment.	

To obtain a distinction grade

To obtain a distinction you must prove that you can make a reasoned judgement based on appropriate evidence.

Command words for a distinction	Meaning
Analyse	Identify the key factors, show how they are linked and explain the importance and relevance of each.
Assess	Give careful consideration to all the factors or events that apply and identify which are the most important and relevant, with reasons.
Comprehensively explain	Give a very detailed explanation that covers all the relevant points and give reasons for your views or actions.
Critically comment	Give your view after you have considered all the evidence, particularly the importance of both the relevant positive and negative aspects.
Evaluate	Review the information and then bring it together to form a conclusion. Give evidence to support each of your views or statements.
Evaluate critically	Review the information to decide the degree to which something is true, important or valuable. Then assess possible alternatives, taking into account their strengths and weaknesses if they were applied instead. Then give a precise and detailed account to explain your opinion.
Summarise	Identify/review the main, relevant factors and/or arguments so that these are explained in a clear and concise manner.
Examples:	
Assess ten features commonly found on a digital camera.	
Analyse your own ability to carry out effective research for an assignment.	

TOP TIP

Check that you understand *exactly* how to demonstrate each of the learning outcomes specified in the assignment.

Responding positively

Assignments enable you to demonstrate what you know and how you can apply it. You should respond positively to the challenge and give it your best shot. Being well organised and having confidence in your own abilities helps too, and this is covered in the next section.

Key points

- Read instructions carefully so that you don't make mistakes that can easily be avoided, such as only doing part of the set task.
- Note the assignment deadline on your planner and any interim review dates. Schedule work around these dates to make the most of reviews with your tutor.
- Check your centre's policies relating to assignments, such as how to obtain an extension or query a final grade.
- Expect command words and/or the complexity of a task to be different at higher grades, because you have to demonstrate higher-level skills.

TOP TIP

All your assignments will relate to topics you have covered and work you have done in class. They're not meant to be a test to catch you out.

Action points

1 Check your ability to differentiate between different types of command words by doing this activity.
   a) Prepare a brief description of your usual lifestyle (pass level).
   b) Describe and justify your current lifestyle (merit level).
   c) Critically evaluate your current lifestyle (distinction level).

It would be a good idea to check that your answer is accurate and appropriate by showing it to your tutor at your next tutorial.

TOP TIP

When presenting evidence for an assessment, think about the person who will be looking through it. Plan your 'pitch' well and make it easy for the assessor to match your evidence against the grading criteria.

Sample assignment

Note about assignments

All learners are different and will approach their assignments in different ways. The sample assignment that follows shows how one learner answered a brief to achieve pass, merit and distinction level criteria. The learner's work shows just one way in which these grading criteria can be evidenced. There are no standard or set answers. If you produce the required evidence for each task then you will achieve the grading criteria covered by the assignment.

Sample assignment front sheet

Remember that you may be penalised for handing in work late. Always meet deadlines or your final grade might be affected.

Ensure that all the boxes on the front sheet are completed, including your name. Sign the declaration to show the work is yours.

Ask your tutor to give feedback on any draft work before submitting a final version to ensure that you have answered the tasks correctly and in the format required to meet the assessment criteria.

This front sheet must be completed by the learner where appropriate and included with the work submitted for assessment.

Learner name		Assessor name	
Sarah Jackson		Michael Croft	
Date issued	**Completion date**		**Submitted on**
21 October 2010	15 November 2010		15 November 2010
Qualification		**Unit**	
BTEC Level 3 National in Construction and the Built Environment		Unit 1: Health, Safety and Welfare in Construction and the Built Environment	

Assignment title	Health and safety responsibilities at work

In this assignment you will have opportunities to provide evidence against the following criteria. Indicate the page numbers where the evidence can be found.

Criteria reference	To achieve the criteria the evidence must show that the student is able to:	Task no.	Page numbers
P1	outline the roles and responsibilities of people assigned specific health and safety duties at work	1	1–4
P2	outline the legal duties of employees and employers in relation to three pieces of health, safety and welfare legislation relevant to the construction and built environment sector	2	1–4
M1	explain how members of the site construction team interact in terms of their health, safety and welfare roles and responsibilities	3	1–4

Learner declaration

I certify that the work submitted for this assignment is my own and research sources are fully acknowledged.

Learner signature: *Sarah Jackson*   Date: *15 November 2010*

This table informs you of the criteria that are being assessed and allows you to enter the page numbers where you have provided evidence for each criteria.

The work you present must be in your own words. Anything that you have copied and used must be acknowledged with its source.

Ensure that you meet the evidence requirements for each assessed criteria. Ask your tutor if you are unsure whether your evidence meets the criteria as there may be different forms of evidence that are acceptable.

Sample assignment brief

The scenario is essential. It sets the assignment in a real, vocational context.

The title is important. Always structure your work so it fits under this assessment title. Don't stray into other topic areas.

Unit title	Unit 1: Health, Safety and Welfare in Construction and the Built Environment
Qualification	BTEC Level 3 National in Construction and the Built Environment
Start date	21 October 2010
Deadline date	15 November 2010
Assessor	Michael Croft

Assignment title	Health and safety responsibilities at work

The purpose of this assignment is to enable learners to prepare a presentation to new apprentices undertaking a site induction.

Scenario
You have been appointed Assistant Health, Safety and Welfare Advisor to Jambs Construction Ltd, a construction company who are undertaking new building work on the outskirts of your town.

The company has recruited new construction apprentices to work on the site and gain valuable site experience.

You have been asked to prepare a presentation about health and safety responsibilities at work for the new apprentices who are undertaking their on-site induction.

Your presentation could be in the form of handouts, PowerPoint™, verbal presentation, toolbox talk or any other appropriate form of presentation.

Task 1
Outline to the apprentices the roles and responsibilities of people assigned specific health and safety duties at work.

This provides evidence for P1

Task 2
Outline to the apprentices the legal duties of employees and employers in relation to three pieces of health, safety and welfare legislation relevant to the construction and built environment sector.

This provides evidence for P2

Task 3
Explain to the apprentices how members of the site construction team interact in terms of their health, safety and welfare roles and responsibilities.

This provides evidence for M1

You need to *outline* (*summarise*) the roles and responsibilities to meet the targeted grading criteria of P1.

'*Interact*' is the key word here. It must be explained in terms of how members of the construction team work together.

These resources will help you to understand the information and concepts included in the assignment.

Sources of information

Books

Topliss S, Skarratt G and Hurst M – *BTEC National Construction, Building Services Engineering and Civil Engineering Student Book* (BTEC Nationals in Construction 2007) (Heinemann Educational Publishers, 2007) ISBN 9780435499242

Chudley R and Greeno R – *Building Construction Handbook, 7th Edition* (Butterworth-Heinemann, 2008) ISBN 9780750686228

Allen E and Iano J – Fundamentals of Building Construction: Materials and Methods, 5th Edition (John Wiley & Sons, 2008) ISBN 9780470074688

Hands D – *Safe Start: GE 707: Safety Handbook, 2nd Edition* (ConstructionSkills, 2005) ISBN 9781857511093

Hughes, P and Ferrett E – *Introduction to Health and Safety in Construction, 3rd Edition* (Butterworth-Heinemann, 2008) ISBN 9781856175210

St John Holt, A – *Principles of Construction Safety* (WileyBlackwell, 2005) ISBN 9781405134460

Websites

www.hsebooks.co.uk Health and Safety Executive Books

This brief has beeen verified as being fit for purpose				
Assessor	Michael Croft			
Signature	*Michael Croft*	Date	21 October 2010	
Internal verifier	John Peters			
Signature	*John Peters*	Date	21 October 2010	

Sample learner work

Some of the legal duties of the employer have been described. This provides evidence towards P1.

This slide lists those people assigned specific health and safety duties at work and provides evidence towards P1. This should be expanded to look at rights and responsibilities.

This work describes the employee's duties under the Health and Safety at Work Act and provides evidence to meet P1.

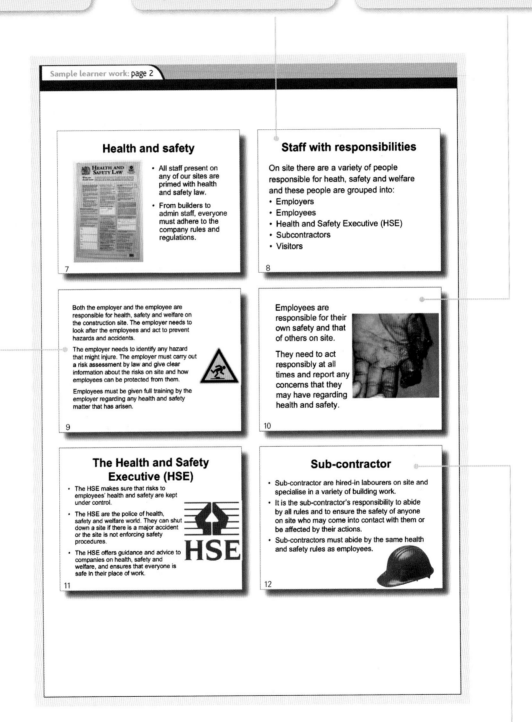

Sample learner work: page 2

Health and safety

- All staff present on any of our sites are primed with health and safety law.
- From builders to admin staff, everyone must adhere to the company rules and regulations.

7

Staff with responsibilities

On site there are a variety of people responsible for heath, safety and welfare and these people are grouped into:
- Employers
- Employees
- Health and Safety Executive (HSE)
- Subcontractors
- Visitors

8

Both the employer and the employee are responsible for health, safety and welfare on the construction site. The employer needs to look after the employees and act to prevent hazards and accidents.

The employer needs to identify any hazard that might injure. The employer must carry out a risk assessment by law and give clear information about the risks on site and how employees can be protected from them.

Employees must be given full training by the employer regarding any health and safety matter that has arisen.

9

Employees are responsible for their own safety and that of others on site.

They need to act responsibly at all times and report any concerns that they may have regarding health and safety.

10

The Health and Safety Executive (HSE)

- The HSE makes sure that risks to employees' health and safety are kept under control.
- The HSE are the police of health, safety and welfare world. They can shut down a site if there is a major accident or the site is not enforcing safety procedures.
- The HSE offers guidance and advice to companies on health, safety and welfare, and ensures that everyone is safe in their place of work.

11

Sub-contractor

- Sub-contractor are hired-in labourers on site and specialise in a variety of building work.
- It is the sub-contractor's responsibility to abide by all rules and to ensure the safety of anyone on site who may come into contact with them or be affected by their actions.
- Sub-contractors must abide by the same health and safety rules as employees.

12

The health and safety role of the sub-contractor has been outlined. This provides evidence towards P1.

'Visitors' is a good topic for health and safety at work, as it covers inductions, safety briefings and PPE. The topic provides more evidence towards P1.

Three good pieces of health and safety legislation have been identified, but only two mention employer and employee's brief duties.

This description of the HASWA 1974 does not contain the duties of employers or employees and is not suitable evidence to meet P2. However these duties were explained in the verbal presentation which was witnessed by the tutor, meeting P2 in full.

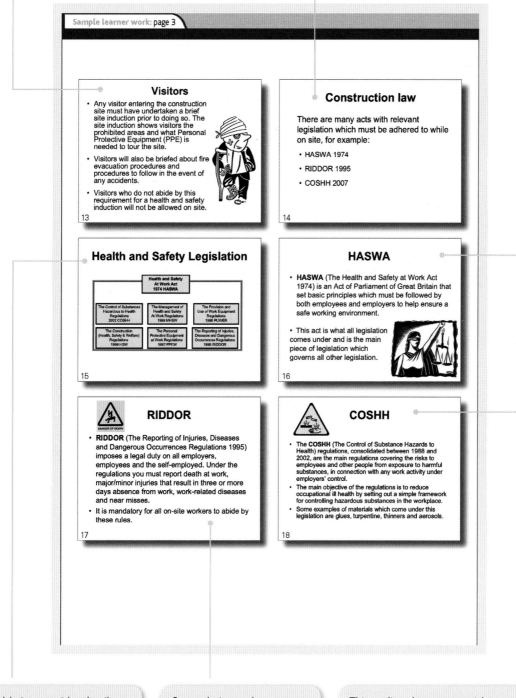

Sample learner work: page 3

Visitors

- Any visitor entering the construction site must have undertaken a brief site induction prior to doing so. The site induction shows visitors the prohibited areas and what Personal Protective Equipment (PPE) is needed to tour the site.
- Visitors will also be briefed about fire evacuation procedures and procedures to follow in the event of any accidents.
- Visitors who do not abide by this requirement for a health and safety induction will not be allowed on site.

13

Construction law

There are many acts with relevant legislation which must be adhered to while on site, for example:

- HASWA 1974
- RIDDOR 1995
- COSHH 2007

14

Health and Safety Legislation

[table: Health and Safety At Work Act 1974 HASWA; The Control of Substances Hazardous to Health Regulations 2002 COSHH; The Management of Health and Safety At Work Regulations 1999 MHSW; The Provision and Use of Work Equipment Regulations 1998 PUWER; The Construction (Health, Safety & Welfare) Regulations 1996 HSW; The Personal Protective Equipment at Work Regulations 1992 PPEW; The Reporting of Injuries, Diseases and Dangerous Occurrences Regulations 1995 RIDDOR]

15

HASWA

- **HASWA** (The Health and Safety at Work Act 1974) is an Act of Parliament of Great Britain that set basic principles which must be followed by both employees and employers to help ensure a safe working environment.
- This act is what all legislation comes under and is the main piece of legislation which governs all other legislation.

16

RIDDOR

- **RIDDOR** (The Reporting of Injuries, Diseases and Dangerous Occurrences Regulations 1995) imposes a legal duty on all employers, employees and the self-employed. Under the regulations you must report death at work, major/minor injuries that result in three or more days absence from work, work-related diseases and near misses.
- It is mandatory for all on-site workers to abide by these rules.

17

COSHH

- The **COSHH** (The Control of Substance Hazards to Health) regulations, consolidated between 1988 and 2002, are the main regulations covering the risks to employees and other people from exposure to harmful substances, in connection with any work activity under employers' control.
- The main objective of the regulations is to reduce occupational ill health by setting out a simple framework for controlling hazardous substances in the workplace.
- Some examples of materials which come under this legislation are glues, turpentine, thinners and aerosols.

18

This table just provides details of construction health and safety legislation and does not provide any evidence for P2. However, the learner gave a verbal explanation in the presentation.

Some duties under RIDDOR have been explained. Reporting procedures are shown on the slide, contributing evidence for P2.

This outline does not provide any evidence for employer or employees duties under COSHH Regulations 2002. However, the learner gave a verbal explanation in the presentation. This is evidenced through the tutor observation record.

This slide gives useful information. Details of how members of the construction team interact were given in more detail in the verbal presentation.

Communication between the construction team is a form of interaction. Several different methods of achieving this are illustrated, providing evidence for M1.

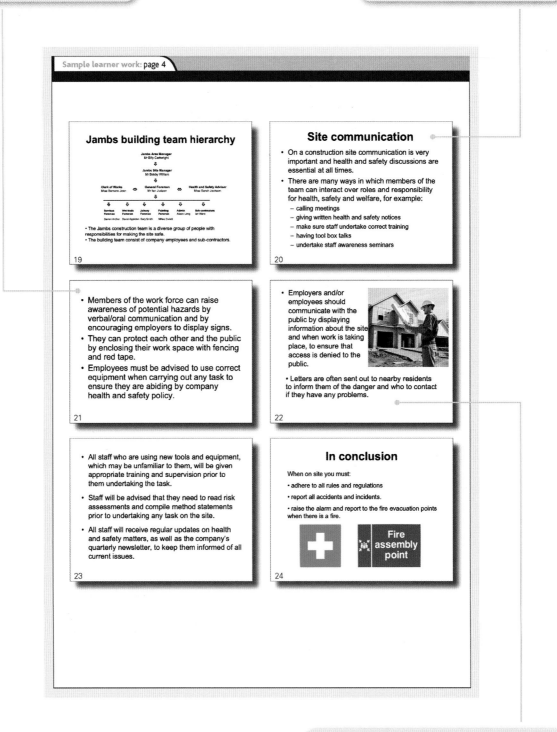

Sample learner work: page 4

Jambs building team hierarchy

Jambs Area Manager
Mr Billy Cartwright
⇩
Jambs Site Manager
Mr Bobby William
⇩

Clerk of Works   General Foreman   Health and Safety Advisor
Miss Samanta Jones   Mr Ian Judson   Miss Sarah Jackson

Services Foreman · Wet trade Foreman · Joinery Foreman · Painting Foreman · Admin Aaron Long · Sub-contractors Ian Ward
Darren Archer · David Appleton · Gary Smith · Miltee Owlett

• The Jambs construction team is a diverse group of people with responsibilities for making the site safe.
• The building team consist of company employees and sub-contractors.

19

Site communication

• On a construction site communication is very important and health and safety discussions are essential at all times.
• There are many ways in which members of the team can interact over roles and responsibility for health, safety and welfare, for example:
  – calling meetings
  – giving written health and safety notices
  – make sure staff undertake correct training
  – having tool box talks
  – undertake staff awareness seminars

20

• Members of the work force can raise awareness of potential hazards by verbal/oral communication and by encouraging employers to display signs.
• They can protect each other and the public by enclosing their work space with fencing and red tape.
• Employees must be advised to use correct equipment when carrying out any task to ensure they are abiding by company health and safety policy.

21

• Employers and/or employees should communicate with the public by displaying information about the site and when work is taking place, to ensure that access is denied to the public.

• Letters are often sent out to nearby residents to inform them of the danger and who to contact if they have any problems.

22

• All staff who are using new tools and equipment, which may be unfamiliar to them, will be given appropriate training and supervision prior to them undertaking the task.

• Staff will be advised that they need to read risk assessments and compile method statements prior to undertaking any task on the site.

• All staff will receive regular updates on health and safety matters, as well as the company's quarterly newsletter, to keep them informed of all current issues.

23

In conclusion

When on site you must:

• adhere to all rules and regulations

• report all accidents and incidents.

• raise the alarm and report to the fire evacuation points when there is a fire.

Fire assembly point

24

This slide provides information on interaction with the public but does not cover interaction within the construction team. This was covered in the verbal presentation and evidence for this is shown in the tutor observation record.

Tutor's observation record

Learner name	Sarah Jackson
Programme	BTEC Level 3 National in Construction and the Built Environment
Unit number and title	Unit 1: Health, Safety and Welfare in Construction and the Built Environment

Description of activity undertaken (please be as specific as possible)

The scenario required Sarah to prepare a presentation about health and safety responsibilities at work for new apprentices undertaking their on-site induction.

Assessment and grading criteria

P1: Outline the roles and responsibilities of people assigned specific health and safety duties at work

P2: Outline the legal duties of employees and employers in relation to three pieces of health, safety and welfare legislation relevant to the construction and the built environment sector

M1: Explain how the members of the site construction team interact in terms of their health, safety and welfare roles and responsibilities

How the activity meets the requirements of the assessment and grading criteria

Sarah's presentation was clear and understandable. She explained the roles and responsibilities of persons assigned specific health and safety duties at work, the legal duties of employees and employers in relation to key pieces of health, safety and welfare legislation, including HASWA 1974, RIDDOR 1995 and COSHH 2007. She also gave a full explanation of health and safety legislation in the Construction industry. Her presentation covered how the members of the building team interact in terms of their health, safety and welfare roles and responsibilities.

Learner signature	Sarah Jackson	Date	15 November 2010
Assessor signature	Michael Croft	Date	15 November 2010
Assessor name	Michael Croft		

The tutor's observation record shows that the learner covered issues in the presentation that were not recorded on the presentation slides

Sample assessor's comments

Make sure that you leave feedback for the assessor. This helps you to think about how you have done and also helps the assessor decide if this method of assessment is working well, or needs to be changed.

This box clearly illustrates whether you have achieved the grading criteria being assessed within this assignment.

Qualification	BTEC Level 3 National in Construction and the Built Environment	Year	2010–2011
Unit number and title	Unit 1: Health, Safety and Welfare in Construction and the Built Environment	Learner name	Sarah Jackson

Grading criteria	Achieved?
P1 outline the roles and responsibilities of people assigned specific health and safety duties at work	Y
P2 outline the legal duties of employees and employers in relation to three pieces of health, safety and welfare legislation relevant to the construction and built environment sector	Y
M1 explain how members of the site construction team interact in terms of their health, safety and welfare roles and responsibilities	Y

Learner feedback

I found this a really engaging and interesting assignment. It was challenging to imagine myself giving a presentation on health and safety for new apprentices. This could be me in just a few years!

Assessor feedback

Good piece of work clearly showing all the grading criteria is met. Clear presentation and knowledge show of subject. Good research for subject. Well done.

Start to collate evidence now for Assignment 2 Risk Assessment.

You show in your final paragraph that you generated enough evidence to obtain the Merit grade which shows you presented work for interaction between workers.

Action plan

Start to collate evidence for Assignment 2 Risk Assessment.

Assessor signature	Michael Croft		Date	17 November 2010
Learner signature	Sarah Jackson		Date	20 November 2010

The action plan is important and will be decided by you and your tutor together. It will help you to identify areas you need to improve on in future assignments.

Step Seven: Work productively as a member of a group

Case study: Working with others

Sunita has finished her studies at school and is moving on to her local further education college – which has a large built environment vocational sector – to study the BTEC Level 3 National in Construction. She had many friends at school, but now they are all studying on different courses or working. Sunita feels very lonely on her first day at college as she doesn't know many people and she finds she is the only girl on the course.

The induction that the tutor has prepared is designed to:

- make learners feel at ease
- enable them to get to know others in the class
- settle them into the new surroundings
- make everyone feel part of a team.

The tutor gives everyone a number and the learners have to move to the corresponding table. Sunita doesn't know why this has been done and is a bit unsettled; she was happy sitting next to someone she vaguely knew.

The tutor then asks each learner to pair up with the person next to them. The learners have to interview each other and then tell the rest of the class all about their partners; their likes and dislikes, hobbies and backgrounds.

On a design project you are likely to meet many different people that you haven't met before, from structural engineers to architects and building service engineers. Initially, you will have to get to know them so you can all work efficiently in a team.

Sunita realises that, if she chooses a construction career, she will have to work well with other people in the construction team. She may not know her fellow team members, might not get on with well with all of them, and there may even be individuals who she just won't like due to personality clashes.

Getting to know new people and learning to work well in a team at college will give Sunita valuable experiences for working in a team on a construction site or in a design office.

Reflection points

How should you behave when working in a team? Think of at least five behaviour traits that a good team player should display.

Think about why a team needs a leader. How would you choose a team leader?

In your private life, you can choose your own friends, whereas at work you are paid to work alongside many people; whether you like them or not.

This applies at school or college too. Hopefully, by now, you've outgrown wanting to only work with your best friends on every project.

You may not be keen on everyone in your team, but you should still be pleasant and co-operative. This may be harder if you are working with a partner than in a large group.

Sometimes you may be the group leader. This may inspire you, or fill you with dread. You won't be expected to develop team-leader skills overnight, but it helps if you know the basics.

First, you should understand how groups and teams work and why good teamwork is considered vital by employers.

Working in groups and teams

If you have a full- or part-time job, you already belong to a working group, or team. At school or college your class is an example of a working group.

All working groups have some common characteristics:

- doing the same type of work – though in the workplace you probably have different roles or responsibilities
- a group leader or supervisor
- a reason for working together, such as studying for the same qualification or tackling an area of work too large for someone to do alone
- group members are dependent on each other in some way; at work you may have to cover someone's workload if they are absent
- group members concentrate on their individual achievements and success.

A team is different. As a team member you have a specific objective to achieve **together** – and this is more important than the goals of individual team members.

TOP TIP

Understanding how groups and teams function will help you be a better team worker and a better team leader.

These are the characteristics of a team.

- Team members have a team goal which is more important than any personal goals.
- Team members have complementary skills so that the team can achieve more than individuals working alone could achieve.
- Work is allocated to play to each person's strengths and talents.
- The team members give each other encouragement and support.
- There is collective responsibility for achieving the goal.

A good team leader acts as facilitator and motivator, and gives practical support and guidance.

Working in a team has many benefits. Team members can learn from each other and combine their skills to do a better job more quickly. Working with other people is often more enjoyable than working alone, too. Many industries rely heavily on efficient group working, from IT teams to health workers and the emergency services.

TOP TIP

Focusing on the task rather than on personalities is the first step in learning to work with different people, whose views may not match your own.

There are many benefits to be gained from working as a team.

Being a good team member

Everyone wants team members who are talented, positive, cheerful and full of energy. These are the key areas to focus on if you wish to be a good team member.

- **Your social skills.** This includes being courteous, treating other people as you wish to be treated, saying 'please' when you want something and thanking people who do you a favour.

- **Your temperament**. Expect people to have different views and opinions from you and don't take offence if someone disagrees with you. If you lose your temper easily, learn to walk away before you say something you may regret.

- **Your communication skills.** This includes talking and listening!

Practise saying what you mean clearly, accurately and succinctly. Be prepared to give good reasons to justify your arguments and ideas.

Allow people to finish what they're saying, without interruption, before you talk. Never shout people down. Think before you speak so that you don't upset people with tactless remarks. If you inadvertently do so, apologise.

- **Your commitment.** Always keep your promises and never let anyone down when they are depending upon you. Always do your fair share of the work, even if you don't agree with all the decisions made by your team. Tell people promptly if you are having problems so there is time to solve them. Be loyal to your team when you're talking to other people.

Being the team leader

It can be difficult to strike a balance between 'leading' the team and working with friends. You need to inspire and motivate your team without being bossy or critical.

Important points to remember about being a team leader

- Lead by example. Stay pleasant, consistent and control your temper, even under pressure.
- Everyone is different. Your ways of working may not always be the best.
- Be prepared to listen and contribute positively to a discussion.
- Encourage quieter team members to join in discussions by asking for their views.
- Be prepared to do whatever you ask other people to do.
- Note down what you say you will do, so that you don't forget.
- Discuss alternatives with people rather than giving orders.
- Be sensitive to other people's feelings. They may have personal problems or issues that affect their behaviour.
- Learn the art of persuasion.
- Act as peacemaker. Help people reach a compromise when necessary.
- Give team members the credit for their hard work or good ideas.
- Admit your mistakes. Look for a positive solution and think about what can be learned for the future, rather than making excuses.
- Praise and encourage team members who are working hard.
- Make criticisms constructively, and in private.
- Be assertive (put forward your point of view firmly) rather than aggressive (attacking other people to defend yourself.)

Some notes of caution about being a team leader

- Try to look pleasant and don't glare at people who interrupt you unexpectedly.
- Never talk about team members behind their backs.
- Don't gossip, exaggerate to make a point, spread rumours, speculate or tell lies.
- Don't expect to get your own way all the time – all good leaders back down on occasion.
- Never criticise any colleagues in front of other people. Speak to them in private and keep it constructive.

TOP TIP

Excellent ideas often come from quiet team members. Encourage everyone to make suggestions so that you don't overlook any valuable contributions.

Key points

- There are many benefits of working in a group or as a team. These include mutual support, companionship and the exchange of ideas.
- You will be expected to work co-operatively with other people at work, and during many course assignments.
- It isn't easy learning to be a team leader. Team leaders should be fair, consistent and pleasant to work with, as well as loyal and sensitive to the needs of team members.

Action points

1 Identify the role of teamwork in your area of study. Identify the team's goal and any factors you think will contribute towards its success.

2 Decide how you would handle each of the following difficult situations if you were the team leader. If you can, discuss your ideas with a friend in your class.

a) The team needs to borrow a college video camera to record an event being held tonight. Your tutor tells you that the one you reserved last week is not working and the rest are out on loan.

b) A member of your team has personal problems so you have given him less work to do. Now you've been accused of having favourites.

c) A team member is constantly letting everyone down because of poor work and non-attendance at group meetings.

d) Two team members have disagreed about how to do a task. You're not bothered how they do it as long as it gets done properly, and by the deadline.

e) A team member becomes very aggressive whenever she is challenged in any way – no matter how mildly.

3 Identify someone who has inspired you because they've been an excellent leader. This could be someone you've met, a fictional character or a famous person. Note down what it is about them that impressed you.

The captain leads and motivates the team to succeed.

Activity: Teamwork skills

Think closely about teamwork and answer the following questions.

What three skills could you bring to a team now?

1

2

3

What three skills do you need to develop in order to make a real impact within a team?

1

2

3

Looking at your answers above, how will you gain the knowledge and understanding in order to develop these new skills? For example, you could read one of the books specified within Edexcel's unit specification or talk to a suitably qualified person about a specific skill.

1

2

3

What would you do if you did not get on with a certain team member?

How would you select members to form a team?

Step Eight: Understand how to research and analyse information

Case study: Independent research

James has just enrolled on the BTEC Level 3 National Diploma in Construction after completing his GCSEs at a local school. He wanted to go to college rather than into the school's sixth form, which he thinks he would find too academic. The further education college can offer him a wider choice of construction-related programmes and career pathways, for example construction, civil engineering and building services.

During his studies at school, James relied on the information and handouts that his teacher gave to the class. He neither visited the library, nor did any extra work towards his GCSEs; he was awarded five C grades. So, James is not very motivated when it comes to finding out information for himself, as, for years, he has depended on teachers to supply what he needs.

On BTEC courses, independent research is required because it:

- provides evidence for answering assessments
- extends your knowledge base
- prepares you for university
- helps to establish that your work is your own.

As part of the induction process, James is shown how to use the library and its online resources. He can also access the same information from home using his PC with his college log-in account and student ID.

James is given his first assignment, which is on 'Construction Health and Safety Legislation', a vital area since the construction industry has many hazards. He has to undertake some research on the Health and Safety at Work Act, 1974. For the first time, he logs on to the online student resource and soon finds some information on this topic.

Showing that you can manage your own research at college will place you in a better position when you are working in a construction environment, where you may have to act and think on your own. Often, construction technicians have to enquire about material products – to ensure that they are to the architect's specification and that they meet health and safety standards.

James needs to practise the valuable skill of carrying out research quickly and efficiently so that he does not waste time. Time on a construction site costs money, through delays and possible errors that have to be corrected.

Reflection point

Think about how you research information. Are your current techniques effective?

As a BTEC Level 3 National learner, you often have to find information for yourself. This skill will be invaluable in your working life, and if you continue your studies at higher education (HE) level. Sometimes the information will give you a better understanding of a topic, at other times you will research to obtain information for a project or assignment. Sometimes you may be so interested in something that you want to find out more without being told to do so!

Whatever your reason, and no matter where your information can be found, there is a good and not so good way to go about the task. This section will help if you can't find what you want, or find too much, or drift aimlessly around a library, or watch a demonstration and don't know what to ask afterwards.

Types of information

There are many types of information and many different sources. Depending on the task, these are the sources you may need to consult.

- **Verbal information.** This includes talking to friends, colleagues at work, members of your family, listening to experts explain what they do, interviewing people, talking to sales reps at an exhibition or customers about a product.

- **Printed information.** This includes information printed in newspapers, journals, magazines, books, posters, workshop manuals, leaflets and catalogues. The type of magazine or newspaper you read may have its own slant on the information, which you may have to take into account (see page 65).

- **Written information.** This includes course notes and handouts, reports and other documents in the workplace. If you want to use written information from work, you must check this is allowed, and that it doesn't contain confidential material such as financial information or staff names and addresses.

- **Graphical information.** This includes illustrations, pictures, cartoons, line drawings, graphs and photographs. Graphics can make something clearer than words alone. For example, a satnav instruction book might contain illustrations to show different procedures.

- **Electronic information.** This includes information from electronic sources such as DVDs, CD-ROMs, searchable databases, websites, podcasts, webinars (**seminars** online), emails and text messages. The huge amount of information available online is both a help and a hindrance. You can find information quickly, but the source may be unreliable, out-of-date, inaccurate or inappropriate (see pages 58–59).

TOP TIP

Too much information is as bad as too little, because it's overwhelming. The trick is to find good quality, relevant information and know when to call a halt to your search.

TOP TIP

Consider all appropriate sources and don't just rely on information found online.

Finding what you need

Spend a few minutes planning what to do before you start looking for information. This can save a lot of time later on.

The following steps will help you to do this.

1 Make sure you understand exactly what it is you need to know so that you don't waste time looking for the wrong thing.

2 Clarify your objectives to narrow down your search. Think about why the information is wanted and how much detail you need. For example, learners studying BTEC Nationals in Engineering and Performing Arts may both be researching 'noise' for their projects but they are likely to need different types of information and use it in different ways.

3 Identify your sources and check you know how to use them. You need to choose sources that are most likely to provide information relevant to your objectives. For example, an Engineering learner might find information on noise emissions in industry journals and by checking out specialist websites.

4 Plan and schedule your research. Theoretically, you could research information forever. Knowing when to call a halt takes skill. Write a schedule that states when you must stop looking and start sorting the information.

5 Store your information safely in a labelled folder. This folder should include printouts or photocopies of articles, notes about events you have attended or observed, photographs you've taken or sketches you've drawn. Divide your information under topic headings to make it easier to find. When you're ready to start work, re-read your assignment brief and select the items that are most closely related to the task you are doing.

TOP TIP

Allocate time for research as part of your assignment task. Take into account any interim deadlines as well as the final deadline for completing the work.

Primary and secondary research, and the law of copyright

There are two ways to research information. One is known as primary research, the other is secondary research.

Primary research

Primary research involves finding new information about an issue or topic. This might include finding out people's views about a product or interviewing an expert. When carrying out interviews, you will need to design a survey or questionnaire. Your primary research might also include observing or experiencing something for yourself, and recording your feelings and observations.

Secondary research

Secondary research involves accessing information that already exists in books, files, newspapers or on CD-ROMs, computer databases or the internet, and assessing it against your objectives.

This information has been prepared by other people and is available to anyone. You can quote from an original work provided you acknowledge the source of your information. You should put this acknowledgement in your text or in the bibliography to your text; do not claim it as your own research. You must include the author's name, year of publication, the title and publisher, or the web address if it is an online article. You should practise listing the sources of articles so

that you feel confident writing a bibliography. Use the guidance sheet issued by your centre to help you. This will illustrate the style your centre recommends. (See also page 66.)

The trick with research is to choose the best technique to achieve your objectives and this may mean using a mix of methods and resources. For example, if you have to comment on an industry event you might go to it, make notes, interview people attending, observe the event (perhaps take a video camera), and read any newspaper reports or online comments.

TOP TIP

Always make sure you make a note of where you get information from (your source). Keep it safely as it can be very difficult later on to work out where it came from!

People as a source of information

If you want to get the most out of interviewing someone, or several people, you need to prepare carefully in advance.

The following points give some general advice about getting the most out of face-to-face interviews.

- Make sure you know what questions to ask to get the information you need.
- Explain why you want the information.
- Don't expect to be told confidential or sensitive information.
- Write clear notes so that you remember who told you what, and when. (See also page 60.)
- Note the contact details of the person you are interviewing and ask whether they mind if you contact them again should you think of anything later or need to clarify your notes.
- Thank them for their help.

If you want to ask a lot of people for their opinion you may want to conduct a survey. You will need to design a questionnaire and analyse the results. This will be easier if you ask for **quantitative** responses – for example yes/no, true/false or ratings on a five-point scale – rather than opinions.

- Give careful thought to your representative sample (people whose opinions are relevant to the topic).
- Decide how many people to survey so that the results mean something.
- Keep the survey relatively short.

- Thank people who complete it.
- Analyse the results, and write up your conclusions promptly.

TOP TIP

Test your questionnaire on volunteers before you 'go live' to check that there are no mistakes and the questions are easy to understand. Make any amendments before you conduct your 'real' survey.

Asking someone who knows a lot about a topic can be informative.

Avoiding pitfalls

Wikipedia is a good online source that covers many topics, and often in some depth. It is popular and free. However, it has an open-content policy, which means that anyone can contribute to and edit entries. People may post information, whether it is correct or not. Wikipedia is moving towards greater checks on entries, but it is still sensible to check out information you find on this site somewhere else.

Apart from inaccuracy, you may find other problems with information you obtain through research, especially material found online.

- **Out-of-date material.** Check the date of everything and keep only the latest version of books, newspapers or magazines. Yesterday's news may be of little use if you are researching something topical.
- **Irrelevant details.** Often, only part of an article will be relevant to your search. For example, if you are forecasting future trends in an area of work, you do not need information about its history or related problems. When learners are struggling, they sometimes 'pad out' answers with irrelevant information. If you've researched properly you can avoid this by having enough relevant information for your purposes.

- **Invalid assumptions.** This means someone has jumped to the wrong conclusion and made 2 + 2 = 5. You might do this if you see two friends chatting and think they are talking about you – whether they are or not! You can avoid problems in this area by double-checking your ideas and getting evidence to support them.

- **Bias.** This is when people hold strong views about a topic, or let their emotions or prejudices affect their judgement. An obvious example is asking a keen football fan for an objective evaluation of their team's performance!

- **Vested interests.** People may argue in a certain way because it's in their own interests to do so. For example, when the Government said Home Information Packs must be prepared for all properties being sold, the Association of Home Information Pack Providers was in favour because it trains the people who prepare the packs. The National Association of Estate Agents and Royal Institution of Chartered Surveyors were not because they thought they would lose business if people were put off selling their houses.

TOP TIP

Don't discard information that is affected by bias or vested interests. Just make it clear you know about the problem and have taken it into account.

Reading for a purpose

You may enjoy reading or you may find it tedious or difficult. If so, it helps to know that there are different ways to read, depending on what you're doing. For example, you wouldn't look for a programme in a TV guide in the same way that you would check an assignment for mistakes. You can save time and find information more easily if you use the best method of reading to suit your purpose. The following are some examples of ways of reading.

- **Skim reading** is used to check new information and get a general overview. To skim a book chapter read the first and last paragraphs, the headings, subheadings and illustrations. It also helps to read the first sentence of each paragraph.

TOP TIP

News articles are written with the key points at the beginning, so concentrate on the first paragraph or two. Feature articles have a general introduction and important information is contained in the main text.

- **Scanning** is used to see whether an article contains something you need – such as key words, dates or technical terms. Focus on capital or initial letters for a name, and figures for a date. Technical terms may be in bold or italics.

- **Light reading** is usually done for pleasure when you are relaxed, for example, reading a magazine article. You may not remember many facts afterwards, so this sort of reading isn't suitable for learning something or assessing its value.

- **Word-by-word reading (proofreading)** is important so that you don't miss anything, such as the dosage instructions for a strong medicine. You should proofread assignments before you submit them.

- **Reading for study (active reading)** means being actively involved so that you understand the information. It is rare to be naturally good at this, so you might have to work to develop this skill.

Developing critical and analytical skills

Developing critical and analytical skills involves looking at information for any flaws in the arguments. These skills are important when you progress to work or higher education (HE), so it's useful to practise them now on your BTEC Level 3 National course.

A useful technique for understanding, analysing, evaluating and remembering what you are reading is **SQ4R**.

SQ4R is an effective method. It consists of six steps.

1 Survey first, to get a general impression. Scan the information to see what it is about, when it was written and by whom. The source, and the reason it was written, may be important. Most newspapers, for example, have their own 'slant' that affects how information is presented.

2 Question your aims for reading this material. What are you hoping to find? What questions are you expecting it to answer?

3 Read the information three or four times. The first time, aim to get a general idea of the content. Use a dictionary to look up any new words. Then read more carefully to really understand what the writer means.

4 Respond by thinking critically about the information and how it relates to the topic you are studying. Does it answer your queries partially, fully or not at all? What information is factual and what is based on opinion? Is there evidence to support these opinions? Is there a reason why the author has taken this standpoint? Do you agree with it? How does it link to other information you have read? What is the opposite argument and is there any evidence to support this? Overall, how useful is this information?

5 Record the information by noting the key points. Use this to refresh your memory, if necessary, rather than re-reading the article.

6 Review your notes against the original to check you have included all important points. If you are also preparing a presentation, reviewing your notes will help you to remember key points more easily.

TOP TIP

SQ4R is just one method of reading for study. Research others and adapt them to suit your own style.

Taking good notes

There are many occasions when you need to take notes, such as when a visiting speaker is talking to your class. There's no point taking notes unless you write them in a way that will allow you to use them later.

Note-taking is a personal activity. Some people prefer to make diagrammatical sketches with key points in boxes linked by arrows; others prefer to write a series of bullet points. You will develop your own style, but the following hints and tips might help you at the start.

- Use A4 lined paper, rather than a notebook, so that you have more space and don't need to turn over so often.
- When you're reading for study, make sure you have a dictionary, pen, notepad and highlighter to hand.
- Leave a wide margin to record your own comments or queries.
- Put a heading at the top, such as the speaker's name and topic, as well as the date.
- If you are making notes from a book or an article, remember SQ4R and read it several times first. Your notes will only be effective if you understand the information.
- Don't write in complete sentences – it takes too long.
- Leave spaces for later additions or corrections.
- Use headings to keep your notes clear and well organised.
- Only write down relevant information, including key words and phrases.

- Highlight, underline or use capitals for essential points.
- Never copy chunks of text – always use your own words.
- Clearly identify quotations, and record your sources, so that you can cite them in your work. (Note the author's name, title, publisher, date and place of publication and the page number.)

TOP TIP

Make sure your information is accurate, up-to-date, relevant and valid. Be aware of bias, and don't confuse fact with opinion.

Key points

- Useful information may be verbal, printed, written, graphical or electronic.
- Effective research means knowing exactly what you are trying to find and where to look. Know how reference media are stored in your library and how to search online. Store important information carefully.
- Primary research is original data you obtain yourself. Secondary research is information prepared by someone else. If you use this, you must quote your sources in a bibliography.
- You can search for information by skimming and scanning, and read in different ways. Reading for study means actively involving yourself with the text, questioning what you are reading and making notes to help your own understanding.
- Read widely around a topic to get different viewpoints. Don't accept everything you read as correct. Think about how it fits with other information you have obtained.
- Taking notes is a personal skill that takes time to develop. Start by using A4 lined pages with a margin, set out your notes clearly and label them. Only record essential information.

Action points

- Working with a friend, look back at the sources of information listed on page 56. For each type, identify examples of information relevant to your course that you could obtain from each source. See how many you can list under each type.
- Check your ability to find the information you need by answering each of the questions in **Activity: Finding information** on the next page. For any questions you get wrong, your first research task is to find out the correct answers as quickly as you can.
- Go to page 88 to find out how to access a website where you can check your ability to skim and scan information, improve your ability to differentiate fact from opinion, summarise text and much more.
- Check your ability to sort fact from opinion and spot vested interests by completing **Activity: Let's give you a tip...** on page 64. Check your ideas with the answers on page 87.

TOP TIP

Make a note of any information that you are struggling to understand so that you can discuss it with your tutor.

Activity: Finding information

Answer the following questions about finding information.

a) Four types of information that are available from the library in your centre, besides books, are:

1

2

3

4

b) When I visit the library, the way to check if a book I want is available is:

c) The difference between borrowing a book on short-term loan and on long-term loan is:

Short-term loan:

Long-term loan:

d) The journals that are stocked by the library that are relevant to my course include:

e) Useful information on the intranet at my centre includes:

f) Searchable databases and online magazines I can access include:

g) The quickest way to check if a book or journal contains the type of information I need is to:

h) The difference between a search engine, a portal, a directory site and a forum is:

i) Bookmarking useful websites means:

j) In addition to suggesting websites, Google can also provide the following types of information:

k) Specialist websites which provide useful information related to my course include:

l) Useful tips I would give to people starting on my course who need to find out information are:

Activity: Let's give you a tip...

In 2009, many businesses were struggling thanks to the credit crunch and falling consumer demand. Some, like Woolworths, closed down altogether. Others laid off staff, or announced wage cuts. Despite this, the Government approved recommendations by the Low Pay Commission to increase the minimum wage rate from October. Although the rise was only small, many unions, including Unison and Usdaw, agreed it was better than a freeze, which had been wanted by the British Chambers of Commerce and the British Retail Consortium.

The Government also announced new laws to stop restaurants and bars using tips to top up staff pay to the minimum level. *The Independent* newspaper claimed its 'fair tips, fair pay' campaign had won the day. It also reported that the British Hospitality Association was claiming this could result in up to 45,000 job losses. The Unite union also carried out a campaign and its General Secretary claimed the decision a triumph for the poorly paid. Not everyone agreed. Some thought there should be no tipping at all, as in Australia. Others said the Canadian system was best – wages are low but generous tips are left, and this motivates staff to give excellent service.

a) Look at the table below. In your view, which of the statements are facts and which are opinions? In each case, justify your view.

Statement	Fact or opinion?	Justification
i) Having a national minimum wage helps low-paid workers.		
ii) Over one million people will benefit from the minimum wage increase.		
iii) The new law on tips will stop restaurants paying below minimum wage rates.		
iv) Using the Australian system of no tips would be better.		
v) The Canadian system guarantees good service.		
vi) 45,000 job losses will occur in the hospitality industry.		

b) All newspapers have their own way of putting forward the news. Go to page 88 to find out how you can access a website which will help you to compare the way that news is reported in different newspapers.

Compare six different newspapers and make notes on:
i) the type of stories covered

ii) the way views are put forward

Activity: How to go about your research

Undertake some independent research to complete the table below. Provide a source for each subject listed that you could use when completing assessments.

Subject	Source (website; book title and ISBN number; article or journal title)
risk assessment legislation	
Level 3 Construction reference book	
RIBA plan of work	
construction lifting equipment	
SMM7	

Make sure that you use the Harvard referencing system when completing the table – you may need to obtain a tutorial on using this system. Here's an example for a book:

Simon Topliss (2007), *BTEC National Construction, Building Services Engineering and Civil Engineering Student Book*. Oxford: Heinemann Educational Publishers.

In this system of referencing, the order of information, punctuation and style of text is as follows:

Author or editor's name (year of publication in brackets), *Book title in italics*. City of publication: Publisher.

Step Nine: Make an effective presentation

Case study: Presentations in the construction industry

Mohammed has been told that he will be taking part in a team presentation on an unfamiliar aspect of construction – the construction of foundations in poor supporting soils and, specifically, the use of piled foundations. Mohammed is not used to speaking in public or in front of his peers and this assignment has been playing on his mind for the last week. Since his fellow team members feel equally inexperienced in public speaking, not one of them is willing to stand up and present.

The course tutor explains to the team that, sometimes in their lives, they will have to speak publically – for example, at an interview, wedding, protest march or public meeting. Construction workers have to speak at construction site meetings to discuss aspects of a project. The assignment is excellent practice and will help develop the required skills. The tutor advises that the first step is to make sure the team members fully understand this complicated foundation subject, which will give them confidence to speak freely.

The tutor suggests that Mohammed's team starts by trying to present in pairs or small groups. The team takes this suggestion on board. After much laughter, which breaks the ice, they are able to speak openly in front of each other. In construction, there is often a pre-contract site meeting, where all parties meet and introduce themselves.

Now that they have tried presenting to one another in small groups, speaking in front of the whole class doesn't seem so bad. The tutor gives each group some time in the lecture room to practise and review their work, and to become familiar with the location and interactive whiteboard, so that the presentations will run smoothly on the day.

The tutor draws lots to decide who will go first – Mohammed's team. They get off to a good start, with an icebreaker that makes everyone laugh, then progress into the main part of the presentation. As they finish the presentation and everyone applauds, the team members sit down ready to listen to the next group. They all realise that the experience wasn't nearly as bad as they had anticipated.

Reflection points

Thinking about your own presentation skills, could you present an idea on a one-to-one basis to another learner? Could you present the same idea to a small group of colleagues?

Given enough time to prepare, could you give a talk to a much larger audience? What about making a presentation to a group of people you don't know?

Making a presentation can be nerve-wracking. It involves several skills, including planning, preparation and communication. It tests your ability to work in a team, speak in public and use IT (normally PowerPoint). You also have to stay calm under pressure. However, as it is excellent practice for your future, you can expect presentations to be a common method of assessing your performance.

TOP TIP

When you're giving a presentation, keep to time, get to the point and use your time well.

You will give better presentations if you note the following points.

Good planning and preparation

Being well prepared, and rehearsing beforehand, helps your confidence and your presentation. The following points will help you to do this.

- If you're part of a team, find out everyone's strengths and weaknesses and divide work fairly taking these into account. Decide how long each person should speak, who should introduce the team and who will summarise at the end.

- Take into account your time-scale, resources and team skills. A simple, clear presentation is better – and safer – than a complicated one.

- If you're using PowerPoint, make slides more interesting by avoiding a series of bulleted lists and including artwork. Print PowerPoint notes for the audience. Use a fuller set of notes for yourself, as a prompt.

- Check the venue and time.

- Decide what to wear and check it's clean and presentable.

- Prepare, check and print your handouts.

- Decide, as a team, the order in which people will speak, bearing in mind the topic.

- Discuss possible questions and how to answer them.

- Rehearse beforehand to check your timings.

If you prepare properly you can really enjoy giving a presentation.

TOP TIP

Rehearsing properly allows you to speak fluently, just glancing at your notes to remind you of the next key point.

On the day, you can achieve a better performance if you:

- arrive in plenty of time
- calm your nerves by taking deep breaths before going in front of your audience
- introduce yourself clearly, and smile at the audience
- avoid reading from your screen or your notes
- explain what you are going to do – especially if giving a demonstration – do it and then review what you've done
- say you will deal with questions at the end of any demonstration
- answer questions honestly – don't exaggerate, guess or waffle
- respond positively to all feedback, which should be used to improve your performance next time.

TOP TIP

Make sure you can be heard clearly by lifting your head and speaking a little more slowly and loudly than normal.

Key points

- When making a presentation, prepare well, don't be too ambitious and have several rehearsals.
- When giving a demonstration, explain first what you are going to do and that you will answer questions at the end.

Case study: Learner quotes about making presentations

Most people start off feeling uncomfortable about talking in front of a group of people, whether they know them or not. This is what some real learners have said about having to give presentations as part of their BTEC course.

"I actually feel more comfortable giving a presentation rather than having to write an essay. What I really enjoy about it is the fact that sometimes we have to prepare a presentation as a whole group. I like that we work together to find information and then we take turns presenting different points. The fact that I am not the only one out there and I am part of a supportive team makes it fun for me."

Gabriela, 16, BTEC Level 2 First in Performing Arts

"Although presentations are very stressful, when I present my work it helps to hang my ideas together and I find I can express what I want to say more clearly than when I write things down. Instant feedback is helpful and boosts my confidence for the next time."

Ethan, 19, BTEC Level 2 First in Creative Media Production

"I think presentations are useful but I find them difficult to deliver – relying heavily on my memory, which is very nerve-racking. We were told that presentation would be part of our assessment. I really worried about it and couldn't sleep the night before – stressing out about what I was going to say. I hated the first few minutes, but after that I was OK."

Will, 16, BTEC Level 2 First in Engineering

"I was very nervous about presenting to my class until I took part in the Young Enterprise scheme and had to present the results of our project to over 200 people including the mayor! After that, presenting to my class mates didn't feel too nerve-wracking at all."

Lizzy, 17, BTEC Level 2 First in Business

"I used to dread presentations on my course, but found that if I went through my notes again and again until I knew the presentation inside out, it made it much easier and the presentations generally went well."

Javinder, 17, BTEC Level 3 National in Construction

"I used to hate presenting to other people on my course, until I realised that most of them were as nervous about it as I was!"

Koichi, 21, BTEC Level 3 National in Art and Design

Activity: All right on the night?

Read the following account and answer the questions that follow. If possible, compare ideas with a friend in your class.

Gemma looked around in exasperation. The team were on the final rehearsal of their presentation and nothing was going right. Amaya seemed to think it was funny. 'Honestly, Gemma, why don't you just chill for a bit?' she suggested. 'You know what they say – a bad dress rehearsal means we'll do really well tomorrow!'

Gemma glared at her. 'Well, can I make a suggestion, too, Amaya,' she retorted. 'Why don't you just concentrate for a change? Sprawling around and dissolving into giggles every five minutes isn't helping either.'

She turned to Adam. 'And I thought you were going to build a simple model,' she said, 'not one that falls apart every time you touch it.'

Adam looked crest-fallen. 'But I wanted to show how it worked.'

'How it's supposed to work, you mean!' raged Gemma, all her worries and anxieties now coming to the fore. 'We'll look stupid if it ends up in bits on the floor tomorrow and Amaya just falls about laughing again.'

'And Imran,' continued Gemma, turning her sights on the last member of the team, 'why is it so difficult for you to count to three minutes? We've agreed over and over again we'll each talk for three minutes and every time you get carried away with the sound of your own voice and talk for twice as long. It just means we're going to overrun and get penalised. And stop trying to wriggle out of answering questions properly. For heaven's sake, if you don't know the answer, how hard is it just to say so?'

Silence fell. No-one looked at each other. Adam fiddled with his model and something else fell off. Amaya wanted to laugh but didn't dare.

Imran was sulking and vowed never to say anything ever again. 'You wait,' he thought. 'Tomorrow I'll race through my part in one minute flat. And then what are you going to do?'

1 Identify the strengths and weaknesses of each member of the presentation team.

Name	Strengths	Weaknesses
Gemma		
Amaya		
Adam		
Imran		

2 What have the team done right, so far, in getting ready for their presentation?

3 Why do you think they are having problems?

4 If you were Gemma's tutor, what advice would you give her at this point?

Activity: Preparing your presentation

Using PowerPoint in presentations can be very effective. The following table gives some prompts that you can use to check you have included the key elements in your presentation.

First fill in the table. Then check your PowerPoint presentation against the completed table to make sure that you have covered everything.

Team name		
Team members	1	
	2	
	3	
	4	
Duties	1	
	2	
	3	
	4	
Introduction • Does the team have a name? • Have all team members been listed on the first slide? • Title slide – photograph? • What are the aims?		
Middle section • What is the main content going to cover? • Format for presenting information? • Do we need animation? • Do we need sound? • Are the colours right? • Is the font size right?		
Summary • What we have learnt? • Conclusions? • Any questions section? • Handouts?		

TOP TIP

When making presentations using PowerPoint, don't just read out what it says on the slides. The audience can do this. Use the slides as prompt cards.

Step Ten: Maximise your opportunities and manage your problems

Case study: Making the most of your opportunities

Max has only just scraped his way into college. He did no revision for his GCSEs, but managed to get C grades in English and Maths. He has previously been excluded from school due to inappropriate behaviour towards the teaching staff. His parents have warned him that, unless his behaviour improves at college, they will no longer support him financially. Max realises that he cannot carry on like this. He has to improve his attitude towards his studies and become more mature.

He has a meeting with his tutor, who explains that learners will be treated like adults but, in return, they are expected to behave like adults. The tutor also points out that, if he behaves badly on a construction site, fellow workers and superiors will not be so tolerant. With all of this in mind, Max starts the course.

After three months of hard work, Max's tutor reviews his progress. Max is delighted with the merit grades he is achieving and he has managed to obtain Saturday employment with a plumbing DIY outlet, which is giving him some experience on the sales counter and a little financial independence. Max now realises

that he must take every opportunity that comes his way, as he will have to compete in the construction employment market in a year's time. Those with better qualifications are most likely to succeed.

Max is expanding his experiences through the Duke of Edinburgh award; not only does Max enjoy the outdoors, but he also knows that the time and effort he puts in will look very good on his CV. Max's parents are very proud of the way he has turned his life round, and of his achievements both at college and in his personal life.

Reflection points

Do you have the confidence to make best use of opportunities presented to you?

Think about a problem you have confronted in the past. How did you tackle it? Do you think you could have done anything differently to deal with this problem more successfully?

If your course takes one or two years to complete, then it is highly likely that you will experience some highs and lows in that time. You may find one or two topics harder than the rest. There may be distractions in your personal life to cope with. All of which means than you may not always be able to do your best.

It is, therefore, sensible to have an action plan to help you cope. It's also wise to plan how to make the best of opportunities for additional

experiences or learning. This section shows you how to do this.

TOP TIP

Because life rarely runs smoothly, it's sensible to capitalise on the opportunities that come your way and have a plan to deal with problems.

Making the most of your opportunities

There will be many opportunities for learning on your course, not all of which will be in school or college. You should prepare for some of the following to maximise the opportunities that each offer.

- **External visits**. Prepare in advance by reading about relevant topics. Make notes when you are there. Write up your notes neatly and file them safely for future reference.

- **Visiting speakers**. Questions can usually be submitted to the speaker in advance. Think carefully about information that you would find helpful. Make notes, unless someone has been appointed to make notes for the whole group. You may be asked to thank the speaker on behalf of your group.

- **Work experience**. If work experience is an essential part of your course, your tutor will help you to organise your placement and tell you about the evidence you need to obtain. You may also get a special logbook in which to record your experiences. Read and re-read the units to which your evidence will apply and make sure you understand the grading criteria and what you need to obtain. Make time to write up your notes, logbook and/or diary every night (if possible), while everything is fresh in your mind.

- **In your own workplace**. If you have a full-time or part-time job, watch for opportunities to find out more about relevant topics that relate to your course, such as health and safety, teamwork, dealing with customers, IT security and communications. Your employer will have had to address all of these issues. Finding out more about these issues will broaden your knowledge and give more depth to your assessment responses.

- **Television, newspapers, podcasts and other information sources**. The media can be an invaluable source of information. Look out for news bulletins relating to your studies, as well as information in topical television programmes – from *The Apprentice* to *Top Gear*. You can also read news headlines online (see page 65). Podcasts are useful, too. It will help if you know what topics you will be studying in the months to come, so you can spot useful opportunities as they arise.

TOP TIP

Remember that you can use online catch-up services, such as the BBC iPlayer or 4oD (for Channel 4 shows) to see TV programmes you have missed recently.

Minimising problems

Hopefully, any problems you experience during your course will only be minor; such as struggling to find an acceptable working method with someone in your team.

You should already know who to talk to about these issues, and who to go to if that person is absent or you would prefer to talk to someone else. If your problems are affecting your work, it's sensible to see your tutor promptly. It is a rare learner who is enthusiastic about every topic and gets on well with everyone else doing the course, so your tutor won't be surprised and will give you useful guidance (in confidence) to help.

TOP TIP

Don't delay talking to someone in confidence if you have a serious problem. If your course tutor is unavailable, talk to another staff member you like and trust.

Other sources of help

If you are unfortunate enough to have a more serious personal problem, the following sources of help may be available in your centre.

- **Professional counselling.** There may be a professional counselling service. If you see a counsellor, nothing you say during the session can be mentioned to another member of staff without your permission.

- **Complaint procedures.** If you have a serious complaint, the first step is to talk to your tutor. If you can't resolve your problem informally, there will be a formal learner complaint procedure. These procedures are used only for serious issues, not for minor difficulties.

- **Appeals procedures.** If you disagree with your final grade for an assignment, check the grading criteria and ask the subject tutor to explain how the grade was awarded. If you are still unhappy, talk to your personal tutor. If you still disagree, you have the right to make a formal appeal.

- **Disciplinary procedures.** These exist for when learners consistently flout a centre's rules and ensure that all learners are dealt with in the same way. Hopefully, you will never get into trouble, but you should make sure that you read these procedures carefully to see what could happen if you did. Remember that being honest and making a swift apology is always the wisest course of action.

- **Serious illness.** Whether this involves you, a family member or a close friend, it could affect your attendance. Discuss the problem with your tutor promptly; you will be missing information from the first day you are absent. There are many solutions in this type of situation – such as sending notes by post and updating you electronically (providing you are well enough to cope with the work).

TOP TIP

It's important to know your centre's procedures for dealing with important issues such as complaints, major illnesses, learner appeals and disciplinary matters.

Key points

- Don't miss opportunities to learn more about relevant topics through external visits, listening to visiting speakers, work experience, being at work or even watching television.

- If you have difficulties or concerns, talk to your tutor, or another appropriate person, promptly to make sure your work isn't affected.

Action points

1 Prepare in advance to maximise your opportunities.
   a) List the opportunities available on your course for obtaining more information and talking to experts. You can check with your tutor to make sure you've identified them all.
   b) Check the content of each unit you will be studying so that you know the main topics and focus of each.
   c) Identify the information that may be relevant to your course on television, on radio, in newspapers and in podcasts.

2 Make sure you know how to cope if you have a serious problem.
   a) Check your centre's procedures so you know who to talk to in a crisis, and who to contact if that person is absent.
   b) Find out where you can get hold of a copy of the main procedures in your centre that might affect you if you have a serious problem. Then read them.

Activity: Achievements and future goals

Complete the table below. In the 'Current' column, describe where you are now in terms of experiences, achievements and qualifications. In the 'Future' column, write about what you intend to achieve in the next two years. The last row is for reflection when you have finished this course.

	Current	Future
Experiences		
Achievements		
Qualifications		
Reflection		

AND FINALLY ...

Refer to this Study Skills Guide whenever you need to remind yourself about something related to your course. Keep it in a safe place so that you can use it whenever you need to refresh your memory. That way, you'll get the very best out of your course – and yourself!

Your Study Skills Guide will help you gain the skills you need for success.

Skills building

This section has been written to help you improve the skills needed to do your best in your assignments. You may be excellent at some skills already, others may need further work. The skills you can expect to demonstrate on your course include:

- your personal, learning and thinking skills (**PLTS**)
- your **functional skills** of ICT, maths/numeracy and English
- your proofreading and document production skills.

Personal, learning and thinking skills (PLTS)

These are the skills, personal qualities and behaviour that enable you to operate more independently, work more confidently with other people and be more effective at work. You'll develop these on your BTEC Level 3 National course through a variety of experiences and as you take on different roles and responsibilities.

The skills are divided into six groups:

1 **Independent enquirers** can process and evaluate information they investigate from different perspectives. They can plan what to do and how to do it, and take into account the consequences of making different decisions.

2 **Creative thinkers** generate and explore different ideas. They make connections between ideas, events and experiences that enable them to be inventive and imaginative.

3 **Reflective learners** can assess themselves and other people. They can evaluate their own strengths and limitations. They set themselves realistic goals, monitor their own performance and welcome feedback.

4 **Team workers** collaborate with other people to achieve common goals. They are fair and considerate to others, whether as a team leader or team member, and take account of different opinions.

5 **Self-managers** are well-organised and show personal responsibility, initiative, creativity and enterprise. They look for new challenges and responsibilities and are flexible when priorities change.

6 **Effective participators** play a full part in the life of their school, college, workplace or wider community by taking responsible action to bring improvements for others as well as themselves.

Action points

1 Many parts of this Study Skills Guide relate to the development of your own personal, learning and thinking skills. For each of the following, suggest the main skill groups to which the chapter relates. Refer to the box above and write a number next to each chapter title below.

a) Use your time wisely. ____

b) Understand how to research and analyse information. ____

c) Work productively as a member of a group. ____

d) Understand yourself. ____

e) Utilise all your resources. ____

f) Maximise your opportunities and manage your problems. ____

2 You have been on your BTEC National course for a few months now and, although everyone is enjoying the work, you realise that some of the learners have complaints.

Firstly, several learners object to an increase in the price of printouts and photocopying, on the basis that they can't do good work for their assignments if this is too expensive. You disagree and think that the prices are reasonable, given the cost of paper.

Secondly, a timetable change means your 2 pm – 4 pm Friday afternoon class has been moved to 9 am – 11 am. Some learners are annoyed and want it changed back, while others are delighted.

a) For the first problem, identify four factors which could indicate that those complaining about the price rise might be justified.

1

2

3

4

b) For the second problem:

i) Think about which learners in your group would be most affected by the timetable change. Who might be most disturbed? Who might benefit from the earlier start?

ii) Try to think of a creative solution, or compromise, that would please both groups.

c) During the discussions about these issues, some quieter members of the class are often shouted down by the more excitable members. Suggest a strategy for dealing with this, which everyone is likely to accept.

You can also check your ideas with the suggestions given on page 87.

3 a) Complete the chart opposite, identifying occasions when you may need to demonstrate personal, learning and thinking skills in your future career. Alternatively, apply each area to a part-time job you are currently doing.

b) Identify areas where you think you are quite strong and put a tick in the 'S' column. Check that you could provide evidence to support this judgement, such as a time when you have demonstrated this skill.

c) Now consider areas where you are not so good and put a cross in the 'W' column.

d) Then practise self-management by identifying two appropriate goals to achieve over the next month and make a note of them in the space provided. If possible, talk through your ideas at your next individual tutorial.

Personal, learning and thinking skills for future career/current part-time job				
Skill group	**Example skills**	**Occasions when you use/ will use skill**	**S**	**W**
Independent enquirers	Finding information Solving problems Making decisions Reconciling conflicting information or views Justifying decisions			
Creative thinkers	Finding imaginative solutions Making original connections Finding new ways to do something Opportunities for being innovative and inventive			
Reflective learners	Goals you may set yourself Reviewing your own progress Encouraging feedback Dealing with setbacks or criticism			
Team workers	Working with others Coping with different views to your own Adapting your behaviour Being fair and considerate			
Self-managers	Being self-starting and showing initiative Dealing positively with changing priorities Organising your own time and resources Dealing with pressure Managing your emotions			
Effective participators	Identifying issues of concern to others Proposing ways forward Identifying improvements for others Influencing other people Putting forward a persuasive argument			
Goals	1			
	2			

Functional skills

Functional skills are practical skills that everyone needs to have in order to study and work effectively. They involve using and applying English, maths and ICT.

Improving your literacy skills

Your written English communication skills

A good vocabulary increases your ability to explain yourself clearly. Work that is presented without spelling and punctuation errors looks professional, and increases the likelihood of someone understanding your intended meaning. Your written communication skills will be tested in many assignments. You should work at improving areas of weakness, such as spelling, punctuation or vocabulary.

Try the following to help you improve your written communication skills:

- Read more as this introduces you to new words, and it will help your spelling.
- Look up new words in a dictionary and try to use them in conversation.
- Use a Thesaurus (you can access one electronically in Word) to find alternatives to words you use a lot, this adds variety to your work.
- Never use words you don't understand in the hope that they sound impressive.
- Write neatly, so people can read what you've written.
- Do crosswords to improve your word power and spelling.
- Improve your punctuation – especially the use of apostrophes – either by using an online programme or by using a communication textbook.
- See page 88 to gain access to some helpful websites.

Verbal and non-verbal communication (NVC) skills

Talking appropriately means using the right words and 'tone'; using the right body language means sending positive signals to reinforce this message – such as smiling at someone when you say 'Hello'. Both verbal and non-verbal communication skills are essential when dealing with people at work.

The following are some hints for successful communication:

- Be polite, tactful and sensitive to other people's feelings.
- Think about the words and phrases that you like to hear, and use them when communicating with other people.
- Use simple language so that people can understand you easily. Explain what you mean, when necessary.
- Speak at the right pace. Don't speak so slowly that everyone loses interest, or so fast that no-one can understand you.
- Speak loudly enough for people to hear you clearly – but don't shout!
- Think about the specific needs of different people – whether you are talking to a senior manager, an important client, a shy colleague or an angry customer.
- Recognise the importance of non-verbal communication (NVC) so that you send positive signals by smiling, making eye contact, giving an encouraging nod or leaning forwards to show interest.
- Read other people's body language to spot if they are anxious or impatient so that you can react appropriately.

> **TOP TIP**
>
> Make sure you use the right tone for the person you're talking to. Would you talk to an adult in the same way you'd talk to a very young child?

Action points

1 To gain access to websites which can help you to improve your literacy skills, go to www. pearsonhotlinks.co.uk, insert the express code 5605S and click on the link for this Action points section.

2 A battery made in China contained the following information.

> **DO NOT CONNECT IMPROPERLY**
>
> **CHARGE OR DISPOSE OF IN FIRE**

a) Can you see any problems with this? Give a reason for your answer.

b) Reword the information so that it is unambiguous.

3 If you ever thought you could completely trust the spellchecker on your computer, type the text given in box A on the next page into your computer. Your spellchecker will not highlight a single error; yet even at a glance you should be able to spot dozens of errors!

Read the passage in box A and try to understand it. Then rewrite it in box B on the next page without spelling, grammatical or punctuation errors. Compare your finished work with the suggested version on page 87.

Box A

Anyone desirable to write books or reports, be they short or long, should strive too maximise they're optimal use of one's English grammar and obliviously there is an need for correct spelling two one should not neglect punctuation neither.

Frequent lea, many people and individuals become confusing or just do not no it, when righting, when words that mean different, when sounding identically, or when pronounced very similar, are knot too bee spelled inn the same whey. The quay two suck seeding is dew care, a lack off witch Leeds too Miss Spellings that mite otherwise of bean a voided. Spell chequers donut find awl missed takes.

Despite all the pitfalls how ever, with practise, patients and the right altitude, any one can soon become a grate writer and speaker, as what I did.

Box B Now rewrite the passage in the space below without errors.

4 In each of the statements listed in the table below suggest what the body language described might mean.

Statement	What might this body language mean?
a) You are talking to your manager when he steps away from you and crosses his arms over his chest.	
b) You are talking to your friend about what she did at the weekend but she's avoiding making eye contact with you.	
c) During a tutorial session, your tutor is constantly tapping his fingers on the arm of his chair.	
d) Whenever you talk to your friend about your next assignment, she bites her lower lip.	

Improving your maths or numeracy skills

If you think numeracy isn't relevant to you, then think again! Numeracy is an essential life skill. If you can't carry out basic calculations accurately then you will have problems, perhaps when you least expect them. You'll often encounter numbers in various contexts – sometimes they will be correctly given, sometimes not. Unless you have a basic understanding about numeracy, you won't be able to tell the difference.

Good numeracy skills will improve your ability to express yourself, especially in assignments and at work. If you have problems, there are strategies that you can practise to help:

- Try to do basic calculations in your head, then check them on a calculator.

- Ask your tutor for help if important calculations give you problems.

- When you are using your computer, use the onscreen calculator (or a spreadsheet package) to do calculations.

- Investigate puzzle sites and brain training software, such as Dr Kageyama's Maths Training by Nintendo.

Action points

1 Go to page 88 to find out how to gain access to websites which can help you to improve your numeracy skills.

2 Try the following task with a friend or family member.

Each of you should write down 36 simple calculations in a list, eg 8 × 6, 19 − 8, 14 + 6.

Exchange lists. See who can answer the most calculations correctly in the shortest time.

3 Figures aren't always what they appear to be. For example, Sophie watches *Who Wants To Be A Millionaire?* She hears Chris Tarrant say that there have been over 500 shows, with 1200 contestants who have each won over £50,000 on average. Five people have won £1 million.

Sophie says she is going to enter because she is almost certain to win more than £50,000 and could even win a million pounds.

a) On the figures given, what is the approximate total of money won over 500 shows (to the nearest £ million)?

b) Assuming that Sophie is chosen to appear on the show, and makes it on air as a contestant, do you think Sophie's argument that she will 'almost certainly' win more than £50,000 is correct? Give a reason for your answer. (The correct answer is on page 88.)

4 You have a part-time job and have been asked to carry out a survey on the usage of the drinks vending machine. You decide to survey 500 people, and find that:

- 225 use the machine to buy one cup of coffee per day only

- 100 use the machine to buy one cup of tea per day only

- 75 use the machine to buy one cup of cold drink per day only

- 50 use the machine to buy one cup of hot chocolate per day only

- the rest are non-users

- the ratio of male to female users is 2:1.

a) How many men in your survey use the machine?

b) How many women in your survey use the machine?

c) Calculate the proportion of the people in your survey that use the machine. Express this as a fraction and as a percentage.

d) What is the ratio of coffee drinkers to tea drinkers in your survey?

e) What is the ratio of coffee drinkers to hot chocolate drinkers in your survey?

f) If people continue to purchase from the machine in the same ratio found in your survey, and last month 1800 cups of coffee were sold, what would you expect the sales of the cold drinks to be?

g) Using the answer to **f)**, if coffee costs 65p and all cold drinks cost 60p, how much would have been spent in total last month on these two items?

Improving your ICT skills

Good ICT skills are an asset in many aspects of your daily life and not just for those studying to be IT practitioners.

The following are ways in which you can Improve your ICT skills:

- Check that you can use the main features of the software packages you need to produce your assignments, eg Word, Excel and PowerPoint.
- Choose a good search engine and learn to use it properly. For more information, go to page 88 to find out how to access a useful website.
- Developing and using your IT skills enables you to enhance your assignments. This may include learning how to import and export text and artwork from one package to another; taking digital photographs and inserting them into your work and/or creating drawings or diagrams by using appropriate software.

Action points

1 Check your basic knowledge of IT terminology by identifying each of these items on your computer screen:

a) taskbar	**f)** scroll bars
b) toolbar	**g)** status bar
c) title bar	**h)** insertion point
d) menu bar	**i)** maximise/
e) mouse pointer	minimise button.

2 Assess your IT skills by identifying the packages and operations you find easy to use and those that you find more difficult. If you use Microsoft Office products (Word, PowerPoint, Access or Excel) you can find out more about improving your skills online. Go to page 88 to find out how to access a useful website for this Action point.

3 Search the internet to find a useful dictionary of IT terms. Bookmark it for future use. Find out the meaning of any of the following terms that you don't know already:

a) portal

b) cached link

c) home page

d) browser

e) firewall

f) HTML

g) URL

h) cookie

i) hyperlink

j) freeware.

Proofreading and document preparation skills

Improving your keyboard, document production and general IT skills can save you hours of time. When you have good skills, the work you produce will be of a far more professional standard.

- Think about learning to touch type. Your centre may have a workshop you can join, or you can use an online program – go to page 88 to find out how to access a useful website that will allow you to test and work on improving your typing skills.

- Obtain correct examples of any document formats you will have to use, such as a report or summary, either from your tutor, the internet or from a textbook.

- Proofread all your work carefully. A spellchecker won't find all your mistakes, so you must read through it yourself as well.

- Make sure your work looks professional by using a suitable typeface and font size, as well as reasonable margins.

- Print your work and store the printouts neatly, so that it stays in perfect condition for when you hand it in.

Action points

1 You can check and improve your typing skills using online typing sites – see link in previous section.

2 Check your ability to create documents by scoring yourself out of 5 for each of the following questions, where 5 is something you can do easily and 0 is something you can't do at all. Then focus on improving every score where you rated yourself 3 or less.

I know how to:

a) create a new document and open a saved document _____

b) use the mouse to click, double-click and drag objects _____

c) use drop-down menus _____

d) customise my toolbars by adding or deleting options _____

e) save and/or print a document _____

f) create folders and sub-folders to organise my work _____

g) move a folder I use regularly to My Places _____

h) amend text in a document _____

i) select, copy, paste and delete information in a document _____

j) quickly find and replace text in a document _____

k) insert special characters _____

l) create a table or insert a diagram in a document _____

m) change the text size, font and colour _____

n) add bold, italics or underscore _____

o) create a bullet or numbered list _____

p) align text left, right or centred _____

q) format pages before they are printed _____

r) proofread a document so that there are no mistakes _____.

Answers

Activity: Let's give you a tip... (page 64)

a) i) Fact
   ii) Opinion – the number cannot be validated
   iii) Fact
   iv) Opinion
   v) Opinion
   vi) Opinion – again the number is estimated

Skills building answers

PLTS Action points (page 77)

1 a) Use your time wisely = **5** Self-managers
  b) Understand how to research and analyse information = **1** Independent enquirers, **5** Self-managers
  c) Work productively as a member of a group = **4** Team workers, **6** Effective participators
  d) Understand yourself = **3** Reflective learners
  e) Utilise all your resources = **5** Self-managers
  f) Maximise your opportunities and manage your problems = **1** Independent enquirers, **2** Creative thinkers, **3** Reflective learners, **5** Self-managers

2 a) Factors to consider in relation to the increased photocopying/printing charges include: the comparative prices charged by other schools/colleges, how often there is a price rise, whether any printing or photocopying at all can be done without charge, whether there are any concessions for special tasks or assignments, the availability of class sets of books/popular library books for loan (which reduces the need for photocopying).

b) i) An earlier start will be more likely to negatively affect those who live further away and who are reliant on public transport, particularly in rural areas. The earlier finish will benefit anyone who has a part-time job that starts on a Friday afternoon or who has after college commitments, such as looking after younger sisters or brothers.

   ii) The scope for compromise would depend on whether there are any classes between 11 am and 2 pm on a Friday, whether tutors had any flexibility and whether the new 9 am – 11 am class could be moved to another time or day.

c) One strategy would be to allow discussion for a set time, ensure everyone had spoken, then put the issue to a vote. The leader should prompt suggestions from quieter members by asking people individually what they think.

Literacy skills action points (pages 81–83)

2 a) The statement reads as if it is acceptable to either charge it or dispose of it in fire.
  b) Do not connect this battery improperly. Do not recharge it and do not dispose of it in fire.

3 Anyone who wishes to write books or reports, whether short or long, should try to use English grammatically. Obviously there is a need for correct spelling, too. Punctuation should also not be neglected.

Frequently, people confuse words with different meanings when they are writing, especially when these sound identical or very similar, even when they must not be spelled in the same way. The key to succeeding is due care, a lack of which leads to misspellings that might otherwise have been avoided. Spellcheckers do not find all mistakes.

Despite all the pitfalls, however, with practice, patience and the right attitude, anyone can soon become a great writer and speaker, like me.

4 (Possible answers)

   a) Stepping backwards and crossing arms across the chest might indicate that your manager is creating a barrier between you and himself. This may be because he is angry with you.

   b) Your friend may be feeling guilty about what she did at the weekend, or not confident that you will approve of what she tells you.

   c) Your tutor might be frustrated as he has many things to do and so wants the tutorial to finish quickly.

   d) Your friend might be anxious about the next assignment or about the time she has to complete it.

Numeracy skills action points (page 84)

3 **a)** £60 million

   b) Sophie's argument is incorrect as £50,000 is an average, i.e. some contestants will win more, but many will win much less. The distribution of prize money is greater at lower amounts because more people win small amounts of money than large amounts – and only five contestants have won the top prize of £1 million.

4 **a)** 300

   b) 150

   c) 9/10ths, 90%

   d) 225 : 100 (= 45 : 20) = 9 : 4

   e) 225 : 50 = 9 : 2

   f) 600

   g) £1350

Accessing website links

Links to various websites are referred to throughout this BTEC Level 3 National Study Skills Guide. To ensure that these links are up-to-date, that they work and that the sites aren't inadvertently linked to any material that could be considered offensive, we have made the links available on our website: www.pearsonhotlinks.co.uk. When you visit the site search for either the title BTEC Level 3 National Study Skills Guide in Construction or ISBN 9781846905605. From here you can gain access to the website links and information on how they can be used to help you with your studies.

Useful terms

Accreditation of Prior Learning (APL)
Some of your previous achievements and experiences may be able to be used to count towards your qualification.

Apprenticeships
Schemes that enable you to work and earn money at the same time as you gain further qualifications (an NVQ award and a technical certificate) and improve your functional skills. Apprentices learn work-based skills relevant to their job role and their chosen industry. See page 88 to find out how to access a website where you can find out more.

Assessment methods
Techniques used to check that your work demonstrates the learning and understanding required for your qualification, such as assignments, case studies and practical tasks.

Assessor
An assessor is the tutor who marks or assesses your work.

Assignment
A complex task or mini-project set to meet specific grading criteria and learning outcomes.

Awarding body
An organisation responsible for devising, assessing and issuing qualifications. The awarding body for all BTEC qualifications is Edexcel.

Credit value
The number of credits attached to your BTEC course. The credit value increases in relation to the length of time you need to complete the course, from 30 credits for a BTEC Level 3 Certificate, 60 credits for a Subsidiary Diploma, 120 credits for a Diploma, up to 180 credits for an Extended Diploma.

Degrees
Higher education qualifications offered by universities and colleges. Foundation degrees take two years to complete; honours degrees may take three years or longer.

Department for Business Innovation and Skills (BIS)
BIS is responsible for further and higher education and skills training, as well as functions related to trade and industry. See page 88 for information on accessing a website to find out more.

Department for Education
The Department for Education is the government department responsible for schools and education, as well as for children's services.

Distance learning
When you learn and/or study for a qualification at home or at work. You communicate with your tutor and/or the centre that organises the course by post, telephone or electronically.

Educational Maintenance Award (EMA)
An EMA is a means-tested award that provides eligible learners under 19, who are studying a full-time course at school or college, with a cash sum of money every week. See page 88 to find out how to access a website where you can find out more.

External verification
Formal checking of the programme by an Edexcel representative that focuses on sampling various assignments to check content, accurate assessment and grading.

Forbidden combinations
There are some qualifications that cannot be taken simultaneously because their content is too similar.

Functional skills
Practical skills in English, maths and ICT that enable people to work confidently, effectively and independently. Level 2 Functional Skills are mapped to the units of BTEC Level 3 National qualifications. They aren't compulsory to achieve on the course, but are of great use.

Grade boundaries
Pre-set points that determine whether you will achieve a pass, merit or distinction as the overall final grade(s) for your qualification.

Grading criteria
The specific evidence you have to demonstrate to obtain a particular grade in the unit.

Grading domains
The main areas of learning that support the learning outcomes. On a BTEC Level 3 National course these are: application of knowledge and understanding; development of practical and technical skills; personal development for occupational roles; application of PLTS and functional skills.

Grading grid
The table in each unit of your qualification specification that sets out what you have to show you can do.

Higher education (HE)
Post-secondary and post-further education, usually provided by universities and colleges.

Higher-level skills
These are skills such as evaluating or critically assessing information. They are more difficult than lower-level skills such as writing a description or making a list. You must be able to demonstrate higher-level skills to achieve a distinction.

Indicative reading
Recommended books and journals whose content is both suitable and relevant for the BTEC unit studied.

Induction
A short programme of events at the start of a course designed to give you essential information, and introduce you to your fellow learners and tutors, so that you can settle down as quickly and easily as possible.

Internal verification
The quality checks carried out by nominated tutors at your school or college to ensure that all assignments are at the right level, cover appropriate learning outcomes and grading criteria, and that all assessors are marking work consistently and to the same standard.

Investors in People (IiP)
A national quality standard that sets a level of good practice for training and developing of people within a business. Participating organisations must demonstrate commitment to achieve the standard.

Learning outcomes
The knowledge and skills you must demonstrate to show that you have effectively learned a unit.

Learning support
Additional help that is available to all learners in a school or college who have learning difficulties or other special needs.

Levels of study
The depth, breadth and complexity of knowledge, understanding and skills required to achieve a qualification, which also determines its level. Level 2 equates to GCSE level and Level 3 equates to A-level. As you successfully achieve one level, you can then progress to the next. BTEC qualifications are offered at Entry Level, then Levels 1, 2, 3, 4 and 5.

Local Education Authority (LEA)
The local government body responsible for providing education for all learners of compulsory school age. The LEA is also responsible for managing the education budget for 16–19 learners in its area.

Mandatory units
These are units that all learners must complete to gain a qualification; in this case a BTEC Level 3 National. Some BTEC qualifications have an over-arching title, eg Construction, but within Construction you can choose different pathways. Your chosen pathway may have additional mandatory units specific to that pathway.

Mentor
A more experienced person who will guide you, and counsel you if you have a problem or difficulty.

Mode of delivery
The way in which a qualification is offered to learners for example, part-time, full-time, as a short course or by distance learning.

National Occupational Standard (NOS)
Statements of the skills, knowledge and understanding you need to develop in order to be competent at a particular job.

National Vocational Qualification (NVQ)
Qualifications that concentrate on the practical skills and knowledge required to do a job competently. They are usually assessed in the workplace and range from Level 1 (the lowest) to Level 5 (the highest).

Nested qualifications

Qualifications that have 'common' units, so that learners can easily progress from one to another by adding on more units.

Ofqual

The public body responsible for regulating qualifications, exams and tests in England.

Optional units

Units on your course from which you may be able to make a choice. They help you specialise your skills, knowledge and understanding and may help progression into work or further education.

Pathway

All BTEC Level 3 National qualifications comprise a small number of mandatory units and a larger number of optional units. These units are grouped into different combinations to provide alternative pathways to achieving the qualification. These pathways are usually linked to different career preferences.

Peer review

This involves feedback on your performance by your peers (members of your team, or class group.) You will also be given an opportunity to review their performance.

Plagiarism

The practice of copying someone else's work, or work from any other sources (eg the internet), and passing it off as your own. This practice is strictly forbidden on all courses.

Personal, learning and thinking skills (PLTS)

The skills, personal qualities and behaviour that improve your ability to work independently. Developing these skills makes you more effective and confident at work. Opportunities for developing these skills are a feature of all BTEC Level 3 National courses. These skills aren't compulsory to achieve on the course, but are of great use to you.

Portfolio

A collection of work compiled by a learner, usually as evidence of learning, to present to an assessor.

Procrastinator

Someone who is forever putting off or delaying work, either because they are lazy or because they have poor organisational skills.

Professional body

An organisation that exists to promote or support a particular profession; for example, the Royal Institute of British Architects (RIBA).

Professional development and training

This involves undertaking activities relevant to your job to increase and/or update your knowledge and skills.

Project

A project is a comprehensive piece of work, which normally involves original research and investigation by an individual or by a team. The findings and results may be presented in writing and summarised as a presentation.

Qualifications and Credit Framework (QCF)

The QCF is a framework for recognising skills and qualifications. It does this by awarding credit for qualifications and units so that they are easier to measure and compare. All BTEC Level 3 National qualifications are part of the QCF.

Qualifications and Curriculum Development Agency (QCDA)

The QCDA is responsible for maintaining and developing the national curriculum, delivering assessments, tests and examinations and reforming qualifications.

Quality assurance

In education, this is the process of continually checking that a course of study is meeting the specific requirements set down by the awarding body.

Sector Skills Councils (SSCs)

The 25 employer-led, independent organisations responsible for improving workforce skills in the UK by identifying skill gaps and improving learning in the workplace. Each council covers a different type of industry.

Semester

Many universities and colleges divide their academic year into two halves or semesters, one from September to January and one from February to July.

Seminar

A learning event involving a group of learners and a tutor, which may be learner-led, and follow research into a topic that has been introduced at an earlier stage.

Study buddy

A person in your group or class who takes notes for you and keeps you informed of important developments if you are absent. You do the same for them in return.

Time-constrained assignment

An assessment you must complete within a fixed time limit.

Tutorial

An individual or small group meeting with your tutor at which you can discuss your current work and other more general course issues. At an individual tutorial, your progress on the course will be discussed and you can raise any concerns or personal worries you may have.

The University and Colleges Admissions Service (UCAS)

UCAS (pronounced 'you-cass') is the central organisation that processes all applications for higher education (HE) courses.

UCAS points

The number of points allocated by UCAS for the qualifications you have obtained. Higher education institutions specify how many points you need to be accepted on the courses they offer. See page 88 to find out how to access a website where you can find out more.

Unit abstract

The summary at the start of each BTEC unit that tells you what the unit is about.

Unit content

Details about the topics covered by the unit and the knowledge and skills you need to complete it.

Unit points

The number of points you gain when you complete a unit. These will depend on the grade you achieve (pass, merit or distinction).

Vocational qualification

Designed to develop knowledge and understanding relevant to a chosen area of work.

Work experience

Time you spend on an employer's premises when you learn about the enterprise, carry out work-based tasks and develop skills and knowledge.

Please note that all information given within these useful terms was correct at the time of going to print.